Bruce VonCannon

Status Anxiety

Hong Kong's Crisis of Identity

palgrave
macmillan

Bruce VonCannon
Vanheel Management Ltd.
Hong Kong, Hong Kong

ISBN 978-981-15-7027-8 ISBN 978-981-15-7028-5 (eBook)
https://doi.org/10.1007/978-981-15-7028-5

This Palgrave Macmillan imprint is published by the registered company Springer Nature Singapore Pte Ltd.
The registered company address is: 152 Beach Road, #21-01/04 Gateway East, Singapore 189721, Singapore

To Phil Davis, who inspired me with the idea for this book,

To Frank Lavin, Dan Kadison, Ed Tiryakian, Pascal Bourqui, and Carter Wrenn for their advice and wise counsel,

To my Cantonese parents-in-law, the late Kim-Foong CHUNG and Shiow-Ing HAN CHUNG for bequeathing their daughter to me in marriage,

To the late Robert Atmore who took a chance on me many years ago when many others were probably more deserving,

Preface

This book is dedicated to the hardworking people of Hong Kong whom I have grown to love and respect during the course of my many years of residency here. My first glimpse of Hong Kong was in 1977 as a post-graduate student studying on a fellowship in Asia. I can remember vividly the plane landing in the late evening at the old Kai Tak airport which was located in the heart of the city off the harbor in the Mongkok district of the Kowloon Peninsula. The feeling as we descended in the plane as I gazed outside my window seat was that of landing in a sea of neon lights. As far as the eye could see there was the glaze of bright, colorful lights. It highlighted the unique aspect of Hong Kong as being the heartbeat of the capitalist world. While there were the standard bright building lights beaming from the top of the major bank buildings and multi-national company offices on Hong Kong island overlooking Victoria Harbor, there were also neon lights over just about every restaurant, medicinal shop, electronics shop, and variety of retail store on every street as far as the eye could see. It left a very powerful first impression. Everyone was promoting their brand!

The enormous *energy* of the people of Hong Kong is in my view its most impressive trait. There might be various interpretations as to the source of that energy, but I doubt anyone who really knows Hong Kong will dispute this outstanding and unique characteristic. Just about everyone who has come to Hong Kong to live and work during the last 70 years has perpetuated this unique trait. They were escaping the perils of the Chinese civil war in 1948–49. They came to Hong Kong fleeing the failed economic and agricultural policies of the late 1950s and early 1960s which had resulted in famine across many areas of China. The flow of people from mainland China continued during the nightmare years the Cultural Revolution 1966–1976. Post-war Vietnam in the 1970s saw the arrival of the "boat people" who risked their lives to escape an economy ravaged by years of continuous war. More recently there were the more professional and technocratic immigrants from China who started coming to Hong Kong taking advantage of the post-1980 open door policy under re-habilitated leader Deng Xiao-Ping. Just about everyone who has come to Hong Kong would admit to coming here to seek opportunity. Some came seeking safety. Others came here to escape poverty and seek a better standard of life. Some came here to seek education for themselves and their children. Their arrival in Hong Kong was preconceived in the notion that they would succeed not by what was to be given to them but, moreover, by a system that rewarded their energy and determination to lead better life. This ability to adapt underscores another Hong Kong trait, that is the trait of *resilience*. This resilience or ability to adapt to changing circumstances and re-invent oneself is a notable Hong Kong trait as well.

That leads to another outstanding trait of Hong Kong and that is the *"rule of law."* It distinguishes Hong Kong from many other jurisdictions within Asia and around the world. The legacy of colonialism, which is a much debated topic with mixed reviews within Hong Kong families, is inescapably intertwined with the history of Hong Kong and has left behind a tradition of "rule of law." This is unmistakable and something that every Hong Konger holds very dear. When one says "rule of law," it should not be mistaken for over-abundance of law or synonymous with a choking bureaucracy. Hong Kong government style is "rule of law," not "rule by law." Most Hong Kongers do not seek a handout. They are conditioned to the idea that one succeeds in life by the law of the farm which says, "one reaps what one sows." This is reflected to some extent by the widely accepted "flat tax rate" enjoyed by Hong Kongers. In Hong Kong individuals pay 16% tax rate and corporations pay 18%. One can almost prepare the annual tax form on the back of a lunch napkin. There are very few (if any) tax loopholes. One is free to work as hard as one wants and everyone pays an equal percentage in taxes on their accrued wealth.

Another unmistakable trait of Hong Kong is the tremendous *diversity* of types of people living within its 400 square miles of territory and among its population of 7.3 million. The population of Hong Kong is 90% Chinese and with the expatriate community accounting for the remaining 10% of the residents of the territory. However, the diversity of this mix of population is stunning. The spectrum of types of people that one might meet on any given day in Hong Kong is another aspect of Hong Kong life that makes it unique and special. Walking down the street on Des Voeux Road in Central District, one is likely to encounter the most cosmopolitan set in the world adorned by the usual accoutrements of wealth and power—men sporting Italian woolen suits and Gucci loafers and Rolex timepieces and attractive women neatly dressed in latest fashion and made up with the finest of cosmetics and sporting Louis Vuitton handbags. However, venturing into other districts of Hong Kong island, or across the harbor on the Kowloon side of the territory, or deeper into the New Territories, one will meet local Hong Kongers who are equally impressive and no less to be admired than the cosmopolites of the business and financial district.

I could wax on indefinitely describing other qualities of Hong Kongers. However, you will discover more of these qualities and attributes in the chapters of this book. I should add that a description of Hong Kong today is not frozen in time. It is not static. It is changing and evolving every day and, in fact, that is one of the prime reasons for writing this book.

Hong Kong
February 2020

Bruce VonCannon

Other Publications by the Author

"The Voice for Reason" (2014–2019 periodical)
"A Guidebook for Today's Asian Investor," (Palgrave-Macmillan, 2017)

For further details see website: www.voncannononline.com

Contents

About the Author

Bruce VonCannon is former CEO of Banque Privee Edmond de Rothschild- Hong Kong and 30 year veteran in the financial industry. In addition to his work and residency in Hong Kong, Bruce's career included assignments in New York, Geneva, Singapore, and Taiwan. He holds a B.A. degree in Politics from Princeton University, an M.B.A. from Indiana University, and a Master's Degree in Agricultural Economics from Purdue University. He was recipient of a Princeton-in-Asia Foundation Fellowship to Nanyang University in Singapore (1976–1978). He and his wife San-San reside in Hong Kong and North Carolina USA.

List of Figures

List of Tables

CHAPTER 1

The House Is on Fire!

Abstract This chapter describes the confluence of forces and events that have tragically brought Hong Kong to the brink of crisis in the second half of 2019. It also underlines the uniqueness of Cantonese culture and how it has slowed the post 1997 assimilation of Hong Kong into People's Republic of China and added to the historical intrigue between Beijing and Guangdong Province and Hong Kong.

Keywords Occupying HK airport · Cantonese diaspora · Dialects of the Chinese · Emperor Qian Long

B. VonCannon, *Status Anxiety*,
https://doi.org/10.1007/978-981-15-7028-5_1

Emperor Qian Long of the Qing Dynasty- grandson of China's greatest emperor, Kangxi, and ruler during the height of Chinese global influence and when the island of Hong Kong was discovered as a mooring area for European traders in the 1790s.

"Sir, please understand we are sorry to inconvenience you."

These were the words uttered to me by a young male university student sporting a surgical mask[1] to hide his facial features in the Hong Kong Chek Lap Kok airport as when I entered Terminal 1 to catch a flight to Singapore for some meetings in the afternoon of August 12th. As soon as I had entered the airport and approached the immigration gate I was surrounded by hundreds of students who corralled me gently in order to prevent me from boarding. I stopped moving and then we all stood around awkwardly in silence sizing each other up for a few minutes (Figs. 1.1, 1.2, and 1.3).

In the background as the minutes ticked by I could hear chants by multiple groups of students now occupying most of the terminal's main lobby which was a large, modern cavernous structure with highly arched glass ceilings about the size of four or five large football fields. In the distance I could discern other passengers being corralled like myself as well and many were shouting at the protestors in frustration. One housewife was crying and pleading to be allowed to join aging parents who had already passed through customs. A few fist fights were breaking out as well. A CNN cameraman and reporter whisked by about 30 feet away in a narrow passage way seemingly to capture the fisticuffs as if to make a good feed for the evening news. The atmosphere was growing more tense by the minute. No police were to be seen in the airport and airport staff had long since abandoned their posts. Chaos was the rule of the moment. However, I instinctively said to myself it is only a matter of time before the riot police reach the airport and I knew that would mean more confrontation. Finally, hoping to defuse the situation with the students I smiled to them and uttered, "I am a bit worried for your safety. This might not end well."

The protestor smiled beneath his mask and replied sheepishly, "We are a bit worried, too. We don't know what will happen. However, we have to do something for the future of Hong Kong."

[1] During the course of writing this book the symbolism of wearing a surgical mask on the streets of Hong Kong evolved dramatically. At the height of the student protests in late 2019, wearing a face mask had become synonymous with resisting the Hong Kong government. For a short period of a few weeks in November and December 2019 it was illegal to wear a mask in public until a court ruling by the Hong Kong Judiciary on December 10th overturned the executive order. As the coronavirus began to sweep across Hong Kong in late January 2020, wearing a mask once again became in vogue but this time accepted by almost all Hong Kongers as an act of promoting good hygiene and as a precaution against the highly contagious nature of Covid-19.

Fig. 1.1 Map of Peoples Republic of China (PRC) (*Source* Chinahighlights.com)

I started writing this book just a few weeks after this encounter at the Hong Kong airport. It had left a deep impression upon me. Civil unrest has an exhilarating impact upon you. It creates the air of uncertainty. It questions the status quo. There is the element of danger, of things being out of control. It stokes fear yet a clinging to the moment, each millisecond. It is the ultimate wake-up call.

The past few months in Hong Kong have been a sensitive time that has created divisions within Hong Kong society. Several times I have asked myself how could one of the world's wealthiest and most modern enclaves have a meltdown like this? What caused it? In the words of Malcolm Gladwell,[2] "what was the tipping point?" For many years I had known Hong Kong to be largely apolitical, a place where people worked hard

[2] Malcolm Gladwell is the author of "The Tipping Point: How Little Things Can Make a Big Difference," a book published in 2000 by Little, Brown which defines a "tipping point" as "the moment of critical mass, the threshold, the boiling point" that are catalysts for significant sociological changes.

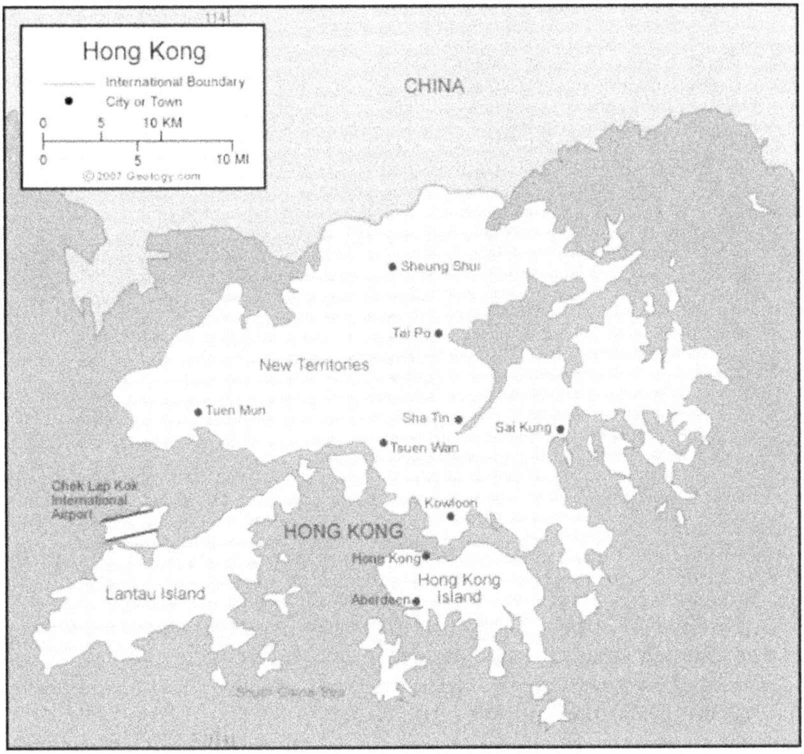

Fig. 1.2 Map of Hong Kong, Special Administrative Region (HK SAR) (*Source* Geology.com)

and just got on with it. It was cool to work hard and pursue the betterment of one's life. I innately gave respect to most Hong Kongers no matter what their stage in life. Working for many years in the wealth management industry in Hong Kong, I had known first-hand the story of so many of Hong Kong's great families. There are so many examples of Hong Kongers who had arrived on the doorstep of Hong Kong's wharf penniless and destitute whom I had personally known who had pulled themselves up by boot-straps to become later in life fabulously affluent, millionaires and respected citizens, and who had within one generation sent their sons and daughters to the best universities in the world. Hong Kong has traditionally been a place that rewarded hard work and one's

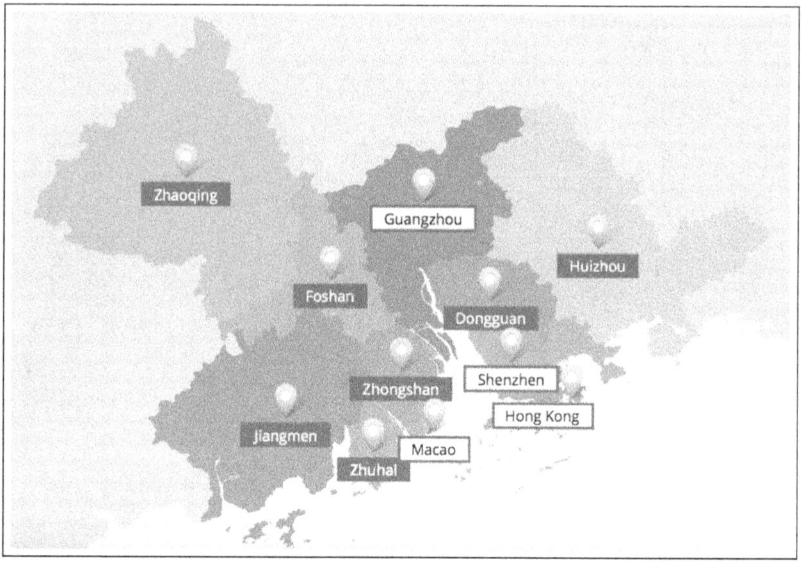

Fig. 1.3 Map of Greater Bay Area (GBA) including nine urban areas of Guangdong Province (Shenzhen, Zhongshan, Zhuhai, Jiangmen, Dongguan, Huizhou, Foshan, Zhaoqing, and Guangzhou (the provincial capital) as well as the two Special Administrative Regions (Hong Kong and Macao)) (*Source* Constitution and Mainland Affairs Bureau, the Hong Kong S.A.R.)

effort to become something better. It was the Asian equivalent for what we called in my childhood "achieving the American Dream." No matter what hand you had been dealt at birth, within a single generation one could build a stable life for a family and more.

However, the protests have changed things. As I progressed in the early weeks writing the book I feared that among my friends many would say "Ah he is pro-government" or alternatively "You see, he is becoming like one of the protesters." My effort throughout this book has been to remain a neutral observer and to be a messenger. In another time and place I might be considered what one used to call in Taiwan "wu dang, wu pai" which sort of means "unaffiliated" or essentially "an independent."[3]

[3] "Wu dang, wu pai" was the affiliation used in Taiwan in the initial period after martial law was lifted in 1987 in Taiwan. Opposition candidates were still not allowed to form

Following the outbreak of tense weeks of street violence in Hong Kong in the second half of 2019, not a single week went by when I did not have conversations with both types of friends, those who had sympathy for the protestors as well as those friends who opposed them totally or at least opposed the violent means by which the protestors were conducting their agenda (quite often the case being the latter). Parents whom I have known for many years have confided in me that their children were out on the streets among the protestors. I also know close friends who are unapologetically pro-government and have wanted Hong Kong Chief Executive Carrie Lam to take stronger measures against the protestors. I also have friends residing in Hong Kong who have told me they feel a coldness directed toward them during the past year because they speak Mandarin Chinese (not Cantonese) at their family dinner table at night. Many have just simply decided to stay home and reduce social commitments throughout the city. One of my friends is in what is called a "mixed cultural marriage" (i.e. one spouse from mainland China, one spouse from Hong Kong) and he confessed to me recently that the latest violence has created strains in the marriage, between the in-laws and between himself and his wife. These have been just a few of the heart wrenching real life stories that I have witnessed. The protests have created divisions within Hong Kong society that may have been below the surface but were for many years repressed out of respect for decency and tolerance for diversity.

On Monday and Tuesday, August 12 and 13 when I was trapped and surrounded by students in the Hong Kong International airport at Chek Lap Kok on two consecutive days as I attempted to board a plane, I, too, realized that I had become part of story that needed to be told. The memory of those two days has remained seared into my memory for the special moments it provided me for discussion with the students and observations made about the Hong Kong protest movement. Thousands of students descended on the airport on those two days most wearing black shirts (the uniform de rigueur of the protest movement) and surgical masks to cover their facial identity (as many protesters feared reprisals from authorities should their identities be revealed). The chants going on inside the airport ranged from peaceful and sincere to downright hostile and threatening. This induced flashbacks to my

rival political parties prior to 1987. However, candidates who were not ruling KMT party members but wanted to seek political office often labelled themselves "wu dang, wu pai" which literally means "no party, no affiliation."

youth during the Vietnam War period, the last time I could remember witnessing deep hostility by youth toward their government. Rebelliousness aside, I detected numerous examples of idealism and innocence as I chatted with several of the students. Although I was firmly surrounded and the students were physically preventing me from moving forward to the departure immigration entry, most of the students were very polite to me. While I have always remained cynical about U.S. President Donald Trump mis-characterizing the Charlottesville riots in August 2017 when he said, "There were good people on both sides," in the case of the protestors in Hong Kong, I can honestly say "there are good people on both sides." The passion driving the actions of most are sincere and those promoting non-violent and orderly protests outnumber the violent and radical ones. On the side of the Hong Kong Police Force and law enforcement authorities, there are good people, too, who believe they are protecting Hong Kong. It is sad that the actions of a few extremely radical elements among the protestors and a very small handful of undisciplined police officers may have plunged Hong Kong into a cycle of re-occurring violence.

As 2019 drew to a close, Hong Kong had faced six months of steady and predictable outbreaks of weekend protests. While the ages of the more than 6000 arrested for vandalism and illegal assembly has ranged between 12 and 50 years of age, it appears over two thirds of the active protesters are between the ages of 16 and 25. There were sadly reports of some of the young protesters being paid by groups linked to overseas interests to commit acts of vandalism. The veracity of these reports remains unclear but some videos circulating on You Tube are chilling. The widespread allegiance to the protest movement by Hong Kong youth has become almost cult-like and is evidence of serious disillusionment by youth toward the Hong Kong government. Some of the protests need no funding. When a child aged 15 years old takes to the streets hurling firebombs and smearing graffiti on walls it is likely they are under the undue influence of some slightly older students, perhaps some teachers, or other unofficial mentors. In addition, the facts related to home ownership in Hong Kong are also sobering and a catalyst for unrest. A recent study released by the 16th Annual Demographia International Housing Affordability Survey covering 309 global metropolitan housing markets ranked Hong Kong the least affordable among the 309 urban areas and vastly more expensive than the 2nd least affordable city, Vancouver, followed by Sydney and Melbourne and Los Angeles. In four categories of affordability being labeled "Affordable," "Moderately Unaffordable," "Seriously Unaffordable," and "Severely Unaffordable," Hong Kong placed squarely under a 'Severely Unaffordable" classification. The survey further elaborated on the material deterioration of middle-income affluence in many global metropolitan areas saying, "One of the principal advances of the past two centuries has been the drastic reduction in poverty and the rise of a large middle-class.........At the heart of this trend was increasing home ownership." Another study cited by Demographia was an OECD Report entitled "Under Pressure: the Squeezed Middle-Class," which boldly noted in its passages that owing to housing price dislocation in many global urban centers "there are now signs that this bedrock of our democracies and economic growth is not as stable as in the past."

A 2017 study of Hong Kong's housing crisis by Ken Chu appeared in *South China Morning Post*[4] providing a comparison between the two leading Southeast Asian economic centers of Hong Kong and Singapore. Singapore's population of 5.5 million is slightly smaller than Hong Kong's population of 7.3 million. Furthermore, Singapore's land space is two thirds that of Hong Kong, thereby making it more densely populated than Hong Kong. However, Singapore's assiduous efforts to promote home ownership through its CPF pension program and public Housing Development Board (HDB) have resulted in 91% of Singaporeans owning their residence. By way of comparison Hong Kong home ownership statistics show that less than 50% of residents now own their home. Despite the fact that Singapore is more densely populated than Hong Kong, the average public apartment in Singapore measures 258 square feet compared to 140 square feet in Hong Kong's public housing. With such limited supply of housing all across the territory, Hong Kongers normally must wait 4.7 years to buy a public apartment. More troubling is the number of years a young Hong Konger entering the work force must wait in order to afford the down payment to buy a residence in Hong Kong. Whereas the average Singaporean entering the workforce must save 15 years in order to afford the down payment for a bank loan in order to buy a residence, in Hong Kong during the past decade residential prices have soared to such heights that it now takes the ordinary Hong Konger

[4] Ken Chu is a local Hong Kong based CEO in the hospitality, leisure, and entertainment industries and was featured in an April 4, 2017 article in *South China Morning Post*.

entering the workforce 24 years of salary to pay the down payment for obtaining a bank loan to purchase a starter residence—that is if he or she spent nothing on food or other necessities. The real wait for the average Hong Konger is likely to be way beyond 24 years. With such gloomy statistics in the housing sector, it should be no surprise that the youth of Hong Kong have become embittered by "the system" that has been so beloved to many others in earlier generations before them.

One well-educated mainland banker living here in Hong Kong remarked to me over lunch one day after a particularly tense weekend of street violence in October, "The problem with Hong Kong youth is indeed a major source of the problem for Hong Kong leaders. It will take 20 years to recover."

Where Has It All Gone Wrong?

From my two afternoons in the airport chatting with the student protestors I noted a familiar sequence of slogans being repeated loudly into megaphones in the airport corridors by students:

"Stand up for Freedom"
"Take Back Hong Kong"
"Revolution Now"
"Hong Kong Independence!"
"Five Demands, not one less!"

The harshness of these slogans was hard to disguise. Were this the streets of Paris full of students protesting against the Fifth Republic in May 1968 or the march by the National Mobilization Committee to End the War in Vietnam in Washington DC in the late 1960s I might not have been so surprised. However, this was happening in one of the wealthiest and most modern cities in the world. This was Hong Kong, the heartbeat of capitalism and spiritual land of Taipans and the Nobel House,[5] and it was August 2019. It felt like the house was on fire.

[5] The allegory to Taipan and Nobel House is taken from the two popular bestseller novels written English/Australian novelist, James Clavell, by the name of "Tai-Pan" (1966) and "Nobel House" (1981).

Inside the Cantonese Diaspora

One aspect of the current unrest in Hong Kong that deserves special attention is the unique nature of the Cantonese ethnicity within Chinese culture. On this subject I dare to claim some bragging rights as my wife is the daughter of proud Cantonese parents. While the typical Westerner may view Chinese people as part of a large homogenous whole, among Chinese across mainland China and in overseas Chinese communities around the world there is a strong awareness of the many sub-ethnicities within Chinese culture. The Cantonese command respect among Chinese as one of the more enlightened and industrious ethnic groups within China. Historically they have been more affluent owing to their coastal proximity and exposure to trade and commerce. Their contributions to Chinese history and culture is vast and they have produced famous personalities including the likes of Bruce Lee (gong fu master and film star) and Hop Sing (aka Victor Sen Yung) as Ben Cartwright's cook in 1960s TV western Bonanza. Other famous Cantonese include General Yuan Chong-Huan (of the early 1600s during the late Ming Dynasty), highly regarded HIV researcher and Hong Kong native Dr. Flossie Wong-Staal, and most notably Dr. Sun Yat-Sen, the acknowledged father of modern China who guided China briefly after the fall of the Qing Dynasty in 1911 when it ceased to be an empire and became a republic.

Guangdong Province, located in the southern part of coastal China in the Pearl River Basin, is the original home of Cantonese culture. It boasts a land mass of approximately 69,000 square miles making it slightly larger than the state of Florida in the U.S. and it offers a friendly sub-tropical climate largely similar to Florida as well. While the state of Florida has a population of 21 million people, Guangdong Province differs vastly here as it boasts a population of over 100 million. Guangdong Province's bustling capital city of 13 million, Guangzhou, was formerly called "Canton" in most Western geography and history publications until the Communist Revolution in 1949. Since then the Mandarin dialect pronunciation of the capital city, Guangzhou, has been increasingly used when referring to it. Although Guangdong Province is only 7% of the Chinese population of 1.3 billion today it accounts for roughly 18% of the nation's GDP ranking it the among the most affluent of China's 34 provinces, municipalities, and autonomous regions. Guangdong Province rivals the juggernauts of Shanghai and its adjacent Zhejiang Province (in central China), Chongqing and its proximity to Sichuan Province (in southwest China), and capital city Beijing and its surrounding Hebei Province (in northern China). Just to give the reader an estimation of the level of prosperity in Guangdong Province today, its GDP of USD 2 trillion in 2018 equaled that of the entire country of Russia.

Same Bed, Different Dreams!

Hong Kong borders on Guangdong province and most Hong Kongers identify themselves as being Cantonese and speak Cantonese just like their fellow Cantonese just across the border although with some slight variation in accent. However, an important linguistic transformation has taken place within China during the past 70 years.[6] Mandarin (originally a northern dialect of China and adopted as the national language only after the 1911 overthrow of the Qing) has become the lingua franca used all across China including Guangdong province. One bright example of this phenomenon is the city of Shenzhen, literally a short walk just across the border from the Hong Kong border crossings at Luo Hu or Futien. Both border crossings can be reached from downtown Hong Kong by subway in the same amount of time it takes to go from midtown Manhattan to Kennedy Airport.

Shenzhen was a sleepy village of less than 30,000 residents until the early 1980s. However, once it was designated a Special Economic Zone (SEZ) with tax free incentives by the central government under the reforms of Chinese leader Deng Xiao-Ping in the late 1970s, its population expanded exponentially. As a result, Shenzhen today can almost be described as the "Miami of China." Just as Miami is a city located in the southern United States with so many transplanted migrants from northern regions particularly New York and Canada as well as Latin America and where one does not so often hear southern accents, Shenzhen has attracted many migrants from other parts of China. Today

[6] There are eight major dialects in China and scores of sub-dialects. They are Mandarin (the national language and originally a northern dialect), Cantonese (Yue dialect from Guangdong Province), Shanghainese (Wu dialect from surrounding Zhejiang and Jiangsu Provinces), Minbei (northern Fujian Province), Minnan or Hokkien (spoken in Fujian Province and Taiwan), Xiang (in Hunan and Guangxi Provinces), Gan (in Jiangxi and Hubei Province), and Hakka.

non-native Shenzhen residents outnumber the local residents. In Shenzhen one hears more northern Chinese accents speaking Mandarin than the local Cantonese dialect (see Fig. 1.4, Dialects of the Chinese).

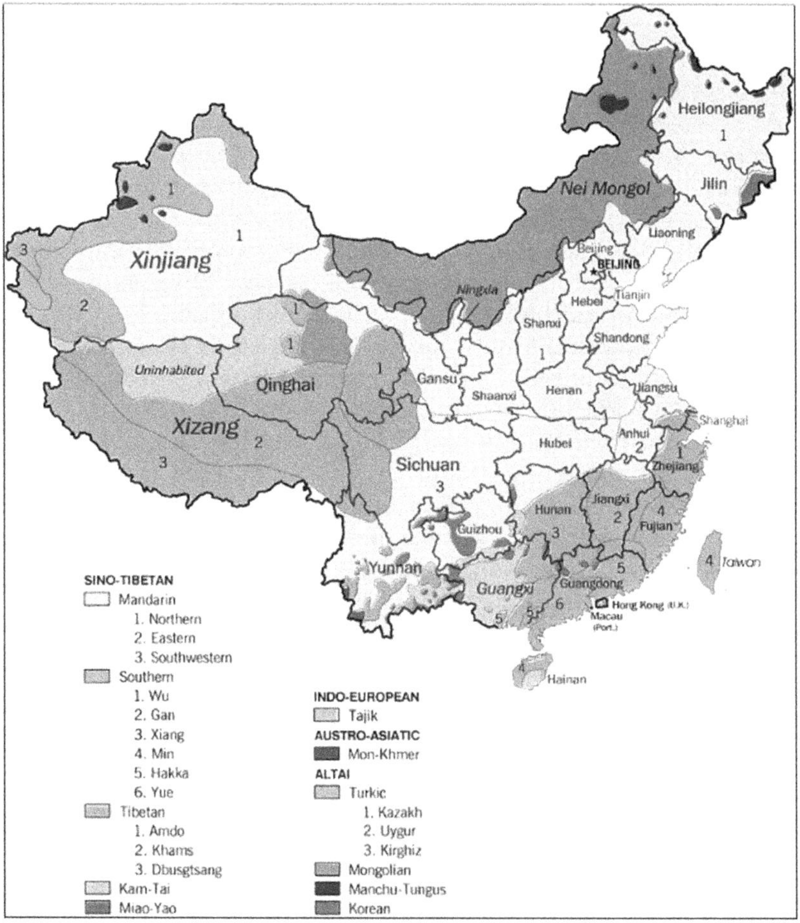

Fig. 1.4 Dialects of the Chinese: Distribution of Linguistic Groups within China's 23 provinces, four municipalities, five autonomous regions, and two special administrative zones (*Source* U.S. Library of Congress)

The success of Shenzhen is staggering and probably without parallel in modern history. During the period between 1980 and 1999 entrepreneurs mainly of Chinese ethnicity set up over 10,000 factory operations in Shenzhen attracting millions of domestic migrants from inland provinces all over China. They arrived in Shenzhen seeking to earn their bounty and fortune. The population of Shenzhen today has swollen to 12.5 million (dwarfing Hong Kong's 7.3 million in just 30 years) including over 25,000 expatriates and it is home to many of China's unicorns[7] including corporate names now known in the West such as Tencent, Ping An Insurance, and Huawei. The GDP of Shenzhen surpassed that of Hong Kong for the first time in 2018. One could almost say "Shenzhen has out Hong Konged Hong Kong!".

One might also take note of the large migration of mainland Chinese who have moved into Hong Kong during the past 22 years since Hong Kong was retroceded back to China from Great Britain. It is estimated that over 1 million mainland Chinese have moved to Hong Kong since 1997. While Cantonese is still the most widely used dialect in Hong Kong, walking down the street at lunchtime in Central District today is quite different from the 1960s and 70s when Hong Kong was almost exclusively a Cantonese speaking city. Today in the Central business district one hears Mandarin dialect being spoken by almost every other pedestrian. The impact of this large migration into Hong Kong has had mixed impact on Hong Kong residents. They both love it and hate it. While China permits an average of 10,000 mainlanders to visit Hong Kong daily in order to boost its tourism and the retail sectors, there has also been a feeling among native Hong Kongers of being overwhelmed. Unlike in the United States where large numbers of migrants particularly from Central America are often impoverished, poorly educated, and lacking medical insurance, many of the mainlanders who have moved to Hong Kong since 1997 are often very well educated, multi-lingual and highly sought after in well-paying jobs in the offices of multinational corporations in Hong Kong's business district.

Notwithstanding the population of 7.3 million living in Hong Kong and the 23 million living in Taiwan, there are roughly 1.3 billion Chinese

[7] A "unicorn" is a start-up company with a valuation in excess of USD 1 billion. CB Insights, a market intelligence firm in the venture capital space, estimated in 2018 that there were 310 unicorns globally with 150 coming from the US and 84 from China followed by the EU (33) and India (14).

living in mainland China. In addition, roughly 30 million Chinese live outside of China in overseas Chinese communities around the world ranging from Singapore, Malaysia, the Philippines, Thailand, Vietnam, and Indonesia to areas in major urban centers like New York, London, Toronto, and Los Angeles. A unique feature of these overseas Chinese communities has been historically they were originally mostly populated by Cantonese.[8] The first Chinese to come to the United States were Cantonese largely during the California Gold Rush in the mid-1800s and a few years later when large numbers were contracted to build the transcontinental railway. However, the landscape has been changing dramatically during the past 25 years. Mandarin has replaced Cantonese as the mother tongue in virtually every overseas Chinese community in North America and Europe. The demographic shift in the overseas Chinese communities started in the 1990s on the heels of investment from Taiwan and China into robust business locations like the Silicon Valley/Bay Area in Northern California and into thriving real estate markets like Los Angeles, Chicago, and New York. Another catalyst for this demographic shift in the overseas Chinese communities has been the staggering growth in Chinese students studying in universities and colleges outside of China. China's "open door policy" the past three decades to allow its students to seek out educational opportunities overseas has resulted in large inflows of well-educated and often affluent Chinese students to universities and colleges in the United States, Canada, the UK, Western Europe, Australia, and New Zealand. Latest 2019 figures showed over 360,000 Chinese students in the United States, 130,000 in Canada, 120,000 in the United Kingdom, 300,000 in Western Europe, and over 200,000 in Australia/ New Zealand. Even in Hong Kong's 22 universities and institutions of higher learning, over 12,000 students from mainland China were enrolled in classes at the outset of 2019, many of them at the elite top universities in Hong Kong.

[8] A few notable exceptions to this Cantonese trend would be the Philippines and Indonesia where a large portion of the Chinese population are Hokkien originating from Fujian Province which lies to the north of Canton Provinces and the location of the old coastal cities of Xiamen, Quanzhou, and Fuzhou. Singapore and Malaysia's Chinese population is dominated by Cantonese and Hokkien ancestry.

"Status Anxiety"

Here are some startling facts:

- Although Hong Kong's GDP has not dropped the past 22 years, its importance to China has become largely diminished with direct travel into China now possible from so many locations in North America and Europe and other parts of Asia. While Hong Kong's GDP has grown robustly in the past three decades and once accounted for close to 27%[9] of China's GDP a mere 25 years ago in 1993, today its GDP only accounts for 2.9% of China's total GDP. With Hong Kong no longer holding a near monopoly on trade going in and out of China as it did from 1949 to 1976 under the British Colonial regime, this has induced a certain "status anxiety."
- Just twenty years ago, Hong Kong's GDP was three times larger than the nine major cities across the border in neighboring Guangdong Province. Today these same nine cities in Guangdong Province aggregately have a GDP three times larger than Hong Kong[10] (see Fig. 1.3).
- With limited land space and high population density Hong Kong's economic vitality is largely dependent upon four sectors: finance, logistics and trading, professional and producer services, and tourism. The reliance on these business sectors increasingly builds the case for Hong Kong to become more closely integrated into the economy across the border into Guangdong Province, a geographical area officially given the name, Greater Bay Area (GBA), by the PRC government's State Council.[11] However, this integration is currently not a strategic aim of those Hong Kongers participating in the recent street protests that began in June 2019. The irony is that, while Hong Kong remains adjacent to one of the hottest pockets of economic vitality in the world today, the young people

[9] Source for this 2017 figure on Hong Kong's GDP relative to that of mainland China is EJ Insight, a Hong Kong based economic journal published by Shun Po Co. Ltd. owned by business magnate, Richard Li.

[10] The nine neighboring urban areas are Shenzhen, Zhuhai, Zhongshan, Dongguan, Guangzhou, Jiangmen, Huizhou, Zhaoqing, and Foshan. Source: Professor Stephen Enright of Hong Kong University, South China Am-Cham Conference, May 2019.

[11] The PRC state council is a 35 member body that is chief administrative authority within China and chaired by the Premier (i.e. Prime Minister).

of Hong Kong have not bought into this dream. Their desperation mirrors that of a generation left behind. Many in the streets have been chanting slogans like "Liberate Hong Kong," "Revolution Now!", and "Take back Hong Kong" as if to have taken a line like "Make America Great Again" from Trump supporters in the United States.

- Other Chinese communities in Asia, using Singapore and Taiwan as examples, have propagated an ethos around public schooling policies that require Chinese learning to be conducted in Mandarin dialect and 18 year old males to serve a compulsory national military service for a period ranging from 1 to 3 years.[12] These measures have in part created a reliable self-defense infrastructure as well as encouraged the development of pride and civic service.[13] The Hong Kong government has adopted none of these policies. So today this first generation of young Hong Kongers in the streets, most of whom were born after retrocession in 1997, are rebelling in desperation and in a manner shocking to many. Sporting British Union Jack and U.S. Stars and Stripes flags in several street demonstrations that raged in late 2019, there is no question that youth in Hong Kong lack pride about being part of China. Many elderly citizens in Hong Kong will point to the fact that Hong Kong does not have to pay for national defense—never under the British (1842–1997) nor under China since 1997. The PRC government does not require Hong Kong youth serve in the military. This has further enabled the Hong Kong government to maintain its low tax regime policies.

[12] After the age of 18 all males in Taiwan and Singapore are required to serve in National Service in either a branch of the army, navy, or air force and then following its completion remain in the military reserve force on standby for a period lasting until 35 years of age.

[13] The Beijing government, like the British Colonial Government, would not likely permit Hong Kong to maintain an autonomous standing military force. Historically, under the colonial government in 1854 a local militia called The Volunteers was formed which eventually became Hong Kong Defence Force (HKVDC) during outbreak of World War II and engaged in bitter fighting against invading Japanese forces. Later in the 1960s HKVDC became the Royal Hong Kong Regiment (RHKR(V)) which served within the 48 Gurkha Infantry Brigade under the command of British forces in Hong Kong. Since retrocession, Hong Kong and Macau residents have been exempt from serving in the People's Liberation Army.

In a global and regional workplace that increasingly rewards language skills in English and Mandarin, many Hong Kong youth do not have a high level of competence in Mandarin. The status quo policies have not prepared them for the future. Many observers of the protests and vandalism ask what is the way out of the current denouement and what solution may be found to de-escalate the street violence in Hong Kong today? Beyond pointing to the obvious shortage of housing in Hong Kong as a key underlying cause of the current crisis, Hong Kong authorities also need a review of language policies in the education system. The official bi-lingual (English- Mandarin) language policy spearheaded by Prime Minister Lee Kuan-Yew in Singapore in the late 1970s has served the island-state well. Prime Minister Lee, a Hakka Chinese himself, may have found it an easier path in Singapore at the time to convert official medium of language learning to Mandarin and English (a bi-lingual policy) than would have been the case in Hong Kong. Singapore's Chinese population has been much more ethnically diverse than Hong Kong's and split between rival Hokkien, Cantonese, Teocheow, Hainanese, and Hakka rival ethnic Chinese communities speaking their respective dialects. In Singapore pushing Mandarin learning actually de-escalated the rivalries within the Chinese ethnic communities. Hong Kong, by comparison has always had a more homogenous Chinese community—90% Cantonese speaking. While Hong Kong education authorities have repeatedly encouraged Mandarin learning in schools since 1997,[14] they have stopped short of implementing draconian methods and preferring to allow some local autonomy and flexibility within the schools.[15] There remains a fierce resistance to Mandarin as medium for learning among certain strata of the Hong Kong population.[16] This remains a delicate area for Hong Kong leadership to address.

[14] A study conducted fifteen years after retrocession in 2012 revealed that Mandarin had overtaken English as the territory's most widely spoken 2nd language with 48% of Hong Kongers able to speak Mandarin compared to 47% being able to speak English (Source: Malcolm Moore, February 24, 2012, *Daily Telegraph*, UK).

[15] Hong Kong Secretary of Education, Kevin Yeung was noted in a radio interview in early 2019 that "the future development of Chinese language learning across the globe will rely mainly on Mandarin" (Source: Thediplomat.com).

[16] Currently 70% of Hong Kong's primary schools use Mandarin as language of instruction. However, it is estimated that close to 90% still speak Cantonese as mother tongue (Source: Kevin T. Bielicki, February 14, 2019, Thediplomat.com).

CHAPTER 2

Hong Kong and the Greater Bay Area

Abstract This chapter takes the reader through the extraordinary rise of Hong Kong from backwater Eighteenth Century trading post to one of the top three global financial centers today and underlines its growing symbiotic relationship between Hong Kong and Shenzhen and the Greater Bay Area (GBA) since the early 1980s. The reader is also exposed to the consequences of the government's economic policy that has regrettably focused too narrowly on economic development at the expense of resolving the growing gap between rich and poor, providing an adequate supply of affordable housing and ultimately the spill over into severe street protests in 2014 and again in 2019.

Keywords Hong Kong global financial center · Top global IPO markets · HK street protests · Greater Bay Area (GBA) · Hong Kong GDP

B. VonCannon, *Status Anxiety*,
https://doi.org/10.1007/978-981-15-7028-5_2

One of the Most Impressive Financial Centers in the World

Hong Kong is the world's third largest financial center and repository for over USD 1.1 trillion (or 16% of all global offshore wealth). In addition to being a booking center where wealthy people store their wealth, there are quite a few wealthy people who live there as well. In 2018 there were close to 250 banks and financial institutions with registered offices in Hong Kong. It is the Asia Pacific headquarters for most of these financial institutions. A handful of financial firms might place their Asia-Pacific headquarters in Japan or Singapore or Australia. However, for the bulk of them, Hong Kong is the preferred location for regional headquarters. Across a survey or other non-financial companies in Asia, they would likewise be inclined to place their Asia-Pacific headquarters in Hong Kong. There are good reasons for such selection. According to a recent Boston Consulting Group study, there are over 173,000 millionaires living in Hong Kong making it a domicile with one of the largest concentrations of wealth in the world. For every 110 families residing in Hong Kong, there is at least one millionaire (Figs. 2.1 and 2.2).

Hong Kong's stock market, the Hong Kong Stock Exchange (HKEX) with over 2400 companies listed, has distinguished itself as one of the elite stock markets in the world today possibly only eclipsed in overall prominence by the stock exchanges in New York and London. According to 2018 figures, Hong Kong has ranked number one globally in 7 of the past 11 years in amount of Initial Public Offering (IPO) funds raised; in fact, number one in three of the past six years (see Fig. 2.3). Hong Kong's stock market capitalization stood at just under USD 4 trillion

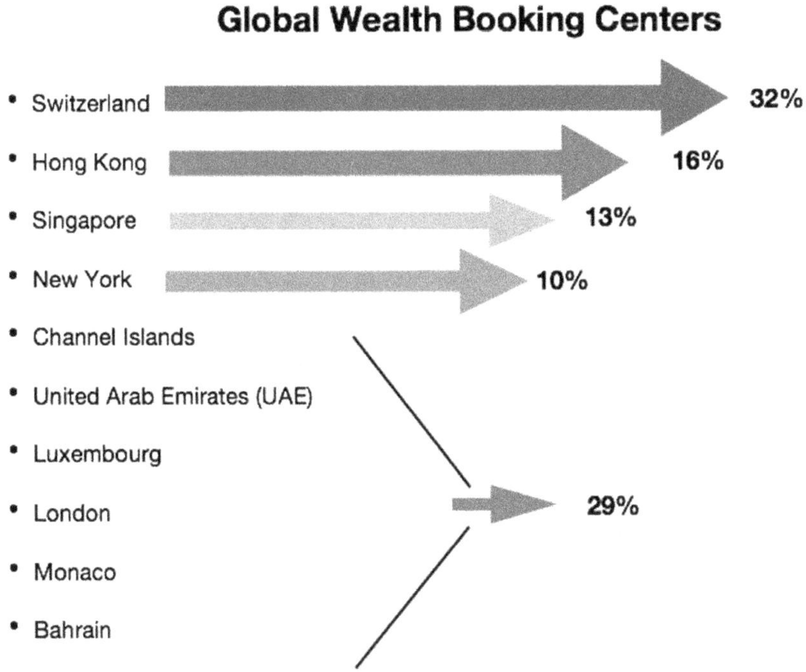

Fig. 2.1 Global wealth booking centers. Through end of 2017 Hong Kong ranked 2nd globally as "booking center" for offshore wealth (*Source* Boston Consulting Group [2018]. The term "booking center" in the wealth management industry refers to the geographical location where the account is legally opened. Switzerland, Hong Kong, Singapore, and New York aggregately comprise 71% of where the world's offshore wealth is stored!)

placing it 5th largest in the world (see Fig. 2.4). The HKEX monthly trading volume averaged USD 182 billion in 2018 making it also the 5th most active market in the world. Such daily trading activity makes it 3 times more active than, let's say, one of its region rivals, the Singapore Stock Exchange. HKEX has long been one of the stock exchanges favored by Chinese company managers for listing their company shares. Over 60% of overseas investor trading comes from either the U.S., U.K., and mainland China. In fact, of that 60% on HKEX approximately one-fifth of the trading comes from mainland China investors. Of the many companies listed on the Hong Kong Hang Seng Index, many are either H-shares or

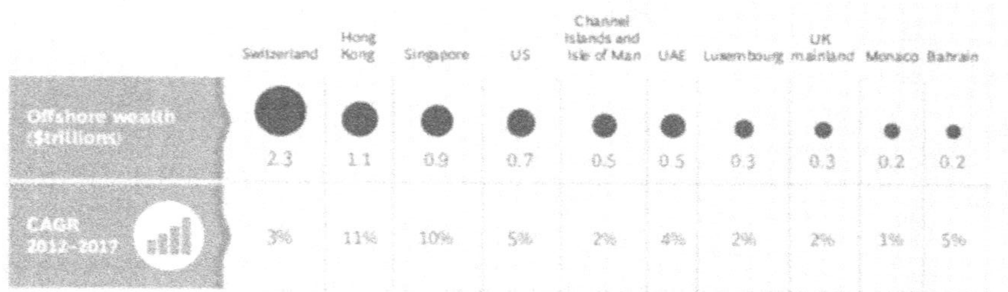

Fig. 2.2 Growth trends in storing offshore wealth 2012–2017. While Switzerland remains the world's number one domicile for storing offshore wealth, through the end of 2018 Hong Kong ranked number two globally and was the fastest growing "booking center" for storing offshore wealth, 2012–2017 (*Source* Boston Consulting Group [2018])

*Top 10 IPO markets of 2019**

Rank	Stock Exchange	Funds raised (US$ billion)	Number of IPOs Issues
1	**Hong Kong mainboard**	**40**	**144**
2	Nasdaq	27.5	133
3	Saudi Stock Exchange	25.6	1
4	New York Stock Exchange	23.4	38
5	Shanghai Stock Exchange	13.3	50
6	Shanghai Star Market	9.5	71
7	London Stock Exchange	7	17
8	Shenzhen Small & Medium Enterprise	4.6	25
9	Shenzhen ChiNext	4.2	52
10	Frankfurt Stock Exchange	4.2	5

Source: Refinitiv **Until December 26, 2019* SCMP

Fig. 2.3 Top 10 IPO markets of 2019. Hong Kong as Asia financial hub and world's top listing venue—Hong Kong ranked no. 1 again in 2019 (*Source* Refinitiv)

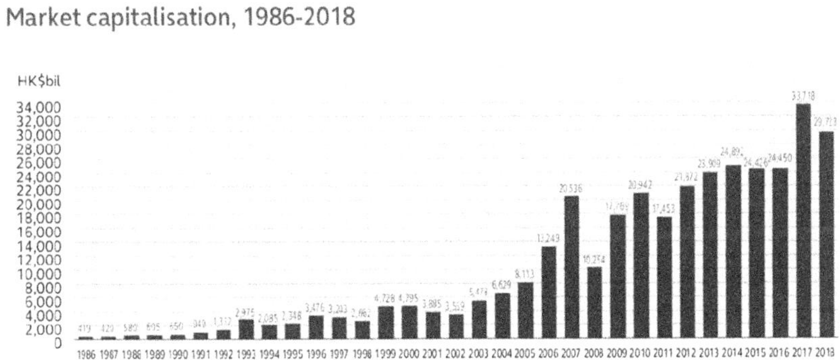

Fig. 2.4 Staggering growth of stock exchange of Hong Kong since the 1980s—From USD 54 billion equivalent to USD 3.9 trillion! (*Source* HKEx Publication [2019])

Red Chips. H-Shares are defined as being mainland Chinese companies who have sought to list their shares internationally by coming to Hong Kong to list. A Red Chip is a Hong Kong listed share of a company whose chief business activities are based in mainland China. This demonstrates the attraction that the Hong Kong stock market has held in the eyes of Beijing as a place to raise capital for the growth and expansion of mainland Chinese companies over the past 26 years since Tsingtao Brewery became the first H-share listing in July 1993. Clearly the growing global prowess of mainland Chinese companies is having impact on the Hong Kong stock market as the volume of capital raised from IPO listings in Hong Kong in 2019 hit USD 40 billion and actually surpassed the amount that was raised individually in the IPO market by both Nasdaq and the New York Stock Exchange. In terms of number of listings, 218 companies listed shares on the Hong Kong Exchange in 2018 making it a record year. Owing to the impact of street protests in the second half of 2019, it looked initially like the Hong Kong Stock Exchange performance would dip in 2019. However, a late 4th quarter surge led by the thunderous USD 11 billion listing on the exchange by Alibaba once again pushed Hong Kong's totals for the year to USD 40 billion and into the number one position globally for IPO funds raised.

Hong Kong stock exchange authorities have not been complacent to merely rest upon their laurels. In 2018 HKEX has launched strategic initiatives to encourage listings by companies whom they feel represent new economy and biotech firms. They include encouraging global biotech firms to list in Hong Kong and establishing a biotech index. By late 2019 over 17 biotech firms now appear as listings on the Hong Kong Stock Exchange and Hong Kong ranks as the world's 2nd largest fund raising hub for biotech companies.

A further significant development of Hong Kong's key role in finance in the region and globally has been the establishment of Hong Kong-Shanghai Connect and Hong Kong-Shenzhen Connect in late 2016 which were intended to allow international investors more access into the China market. Essentially it set up a platform by which any fund manager in Hong Kong could buy securities offered in Shanghai and Shenzhen and vice versa. Daily figures are now quoted each day which monitor the amount of Northbound trading as well as Southbound trading.

Foreign exchange is another area of finance in which Hong Kong has global impact. According to the Bank of International Settlements (BIS) over USD 437 billion in daily FX trading volume takes place each day in Hong Kong and places it 4th globally for daily FX trading volume.[1] Its role as a conduit for foreign exchange extends back in history for many years. Even under the Maoist government in the 1950s and 1960s, Hong

[1] According to BIS, London ranks number 1 in daily FX trading volume (USD 2.4 trillion), New York ranks 2nd (USD 1.3 trillion), Singapore ranks 3rd (USD 517 billion), and Hong Kong ranks 4th (USD 437 billion).

Kong served as an FX window for China. More recently Hong Kong's FX volume has been greatly enhanced by its role trading Japanese Yen (averaging 21% of daily volume) as well as the Renminbi (averaging 17%).

Enough cannot be said about how deep the talent is in the finance industry in Hong Kong. In the realm of private banking, asset management, and investment banking, Hong Kong is the beacon for Greater China and Asia (ex-Japan). Most banks place their best international talent in Hong Kong for at least a 2 to 5 year assignment. The local Hong Kong talent in these three sub-sector areas of finance are outstanding and world class. The central bank of Hong Kong, called the Hong Kong Monetary Authority (HKMA) is the envy of many surrounding countries in the Asia-Pacific region. The role of the Hong Kong Securities and Futures Commission (SFC), an independent watchdog over the local securities industry, has also been crucial to Hong Kong's legitimacy in the financial world. The Hong Kong Securities Institute (HKSI) was established in 1997 to raise standards of excellence throughout the financial industry via its offerings of training programs, examinations, and licensing of professionals working in the industry.

It is worth noting that in addition to the superb standing that Hong Kong has enjoyed in the world finance, its figures in tourism, retail and logistics are also impressive. UK Market research firm, Euromonitor International, ranked Hong Kong the world's number one city for international tourism in 2018 with over 29.8 million arrivals ahead of Bangkok, Singapore, and Macau who ranked second, third, and fourth place respectively. No doubt the large bulk of that tourism in recent years has come from mainland China. Observing tourism in Hong Kong over the past four decades reflects the changing trends in affluence in the region. Thirty years ago the largest number of tourists visiting Hong Kong would have been the Japanese. Over time, however, they would be replaced by Taiwanese tourists in the 1990s. In the most recent two decades, visitors from the mainland have become the largest bulk of tourists visiting Hong Kong throughout the year. Hong Kong's retail sector benefits greatly from this steady inflow of tourists. Tourists from other regions also continue to visit Hong Kong throughout the year as well. The legendary Hong Kong Rugby Sevens tournament held in the late March/early April part of the calendar year has become the biggest social event of the year. It is the most famous sporting event of its kind in the world and attracts spectators from over 24 different countries coming from Europe, North and South America, and other parts of Asia. Restaurant and pub owners will tell you it accounts for one-third of their yearly turnover. However, for the other 51 weeks of the year, Chinese tourists from the mainland have become Hong Kong's largest source of tourists.

Life in Hong Kong is also enriched by activities in the arts. Hong Kong boasts a symphony orchestra and it is a popular stopover for overseas orchestras touring the region. The thriving art scene features many small art galleries located in or around the Hollywood Road area on the hill above Central Business district. Art Basel Hong Kong held in the Spring each year competes with the Art Basel and Art Miami as a major stop on the global art collectors' calendar. Christies and Sothebys both maintain active offices in Hong Kong. For the more decadent pleasures, I know first-hand of some of the fine cigar salons and wine shops in the city. In 2007, Hong Kong slashed an 80% import duty on the import of wine and reduced it to zero in 2008. Overnight Hong Kong became not only the leading wine depot in Asia but one of the leading centers for wine distribution in the world. It is no exaggeration to say that Hong Kongers are among the most sophisticated wine connoisseurs in the world. In addition to wine and fine art, Hong Kong also has some of the most active classic car collectors in the world as well which is a surprising statistic given the cost of parking and storing an automobile in Hong Kong. The cost of a daily parking space in downtown Hong Kong normally rents for approximately USD 600 per month.

When the Apple Cart Began to Tip over

The Street Protests That Began in June 2019

A series of weekend demonstrations and riots staged by students and opponents of the current Hong Kong government have impacted nearly all aspects of life in Hong Kong. The unrest was ignited in early June 2019 by the proposed implementation of an "extradition bill" submitted by Hong Kong's de facto head of government, Chief Executive Carrie Lam. The first weekend of the mass demonstrations saw approximately 2 million or approximately one quarter of Hong Kong's residents hit the streets in a largely peaceful demonstration objecting to plans to present the bill for passage by Hong Kong's Legislative Council (referred to locally as "Legco"). The mass demonstrations, however, morphed over a series of ensuing weekends into widespread violence by radical elements within the protesters. On July 1st, the protestors stormed Legco and heavily damaged the meeting chamber of Hong Kong's largest legislative body. The increasing level of violence was met by armed police who increasingly resorted to using tear gas and rubber bullets to contain the violence that has spread to over a dozen of Hong Kong's urban districts within its 428 square mile area. As the protests became more violent, the police were forced to use stronger and stronger measures to contain the unrest. By mid-August over 700 protesters aged between 16 and 45 had been arrested. While no direct deaths had occurred up until this point in time, scores of protesters and police had been injured in the clashes.

Meanwhile, Chinese authorities in Beijing began monitoring the violence and unrest with increasing alarm. When the protestors rushed the Hong Kong International Airport on August 12 and 13, operations and flights were practically shut down for two consecutive days. The Hong Kong stock market fell by over 7% in the ensuing two days after the airport unrest and regional and global markets were also affected. By mid-week China began a series of media announcements informing the public that preparations had been laid to conduct intervention by a paramilitary force should the situation on Hong Kong streets continue to deteriorate. The thought of military intervention to control the protests casts shivers down the spine of everyone in Hong Kong. The last time massive armed intervention against students by Beijing occurred, an estimated 10,000 students were killed by Chinese troops in Beijing's Tiananmen Square in June 1989. Furthermore, the last time military intervention occurred in Hong Kong on a large scale was mandated by the British Colonial government during 1966 and 1967. At that time British Troops were mobilized to quell riots incited by leftist elements who were largely inspired by the Cultural Revolution which was fully underway in mainland China. Historical records show that by the end of 1967 over 50 people had died (many from incendiary bombs), over 800 had been injured, and in excess of 4000 protesters had been arrested with many later tried and convicted in colonial court (Fig. 2.5).[2]

[2] The 1966 riots in Hong Kong began as a protest against ticket price increases on one of the key transportation links, the cross-harbor Hong Kong Star Ferry an "anti-colonial" movement. The Star Ferry traverses Hong Kong harbor throughout every day every 12 minutes. The protests quickly transformed into an "anti-colonial" movement.

Fig. 2.5 British Troops on the streets of Hong Kong to quell leftist riots in 1967

The Bigger Picture

Hong Kong was formally a British Colony for 150 years until 1997. It was leased to Great Britain at the Treaty of Nanking (1842) in the aftermath of the First Opium War in (1839–1842) when China was under the rule of Emperor Dao Guang, the 6th ruler of China under the Qing Dynasty which had become increasingly beset by corruption in the last years of Emperor Qian Long's reign in the 1790s. A Second Opium war would be fought between 1856 and 1860 which pitted China against Great Britain but also enjoined this time in the fight by the French. The Qing Dynasty would suffer further humiliation. The Treaty of Tientsin (today called Tianjin) in 1858 resulted in further concessions by the Qing Dynasty in the form of opening an additional 10 treaty ports to foreign trade and in total 23 foreign concessions to European powers including France, Great Britain, Germany, and Russia. Thus, began a humiliating period of history for China lasting into the Twentieth Century. The British would eventually fulfill their promise and return Hong Kong in 1997 (Figs. 2.6, 2.7, and 2.8).

Fig. 2.6 Emperor Dao Guang, 6th Qing Emperor (1820–1850). Emperor Dao Guang (Fig. 2.6) was the 6th Qing Emperor to rule China (1820–1850). He ascended to the throne at the age of 38 during a period when the empire had started to decline owing to growing internal strife. Opium addiction was clearly having harmful impact on society throughout China. His personally appointed emissary to Canton (Guangzhou), scholar-official Lin Zexu (Fig. 2.7), insisted upon a ban on opium imports and conducted tense negotiations with the British. War broke out in September 1839 and Chinese maritime naval technology was no match for the ascending global naval power of Great Britain

From 1842 if one will fast forward to 1949 just after the Communist Party seized power in China and the founding of the People Republic of China (PRC) it serves as a suitable inflection point for understanding the Hong Kong that we know today. Hong Kong was just a sleepy British colonial outpost of just under 1.9 million until 1949. Following

Fig. 2.7 Scholar-official Lin Zexu of the Qing Dynasty

the 1949 revolution, Hong Kong's population swelled rapidly with thousands of refugees fleeing across the border from mainland China after the communist regime established control in Beijing. It resulted in the almost doubling of the Hong Kong population between the years of 1950 and 1960. During the 1960s, Hong Kong briefly overtook Shanghai as the epicenter in Greater China of business activity while Shanghai and the rest of the mainland of China stood still sinking into economic stagnation under failed agricultural policies under Maoist rule and the disintegration into a near civil war during the Cultural Revolution (1966–1976). Economic activity in mainland China nearly ceased during this period of history and it is estimated up to 30 million people died of starvation during the years of famine (1958–1962).

Meanwhile, in Hong Kong an economic boom was clearly underway by the early 1970s and similar wealth creation was underway in the regional economies of neighboring Taiwan, South Korea, and Singapore. These four areas in Asia became commonly referred at time as the "four

Fig. 2.8 Sir Henry Pottinger, first Hong Kong Governor (1843–1844). Sir Henry Pottinger, a career soldier from Anglo-Irish heritage, was the British Crown's first appointed Hong Kong Governor. Selected by controversial British Foreign Secretary Lord Palmerston he was to serve until 1844 and then followed by 27 appointed Governors until Hong Kong's retrocession in 1997

tigers" in tribute to their booming economies. Annual GDP expansion in Hong Kong and the other "tiger economies" grew at a near double digit pace throughout the 1970s and early 1980s.

Following the death of paramount leader Mao Tse-Tung in 1976 and the arrest of Mao's wife, Jiang Qing, and the Gang of Four, Deng Xiao-Ping and his followers were re-habilitated politically in China. It was under Deng's monumental market reforms that China re-entered the global economy by 1980. Hong Kong also played a key role in the re-emergence of China's economy during this pivotal time period when the Deng reforms were introduced. However, the role that Hong Kong has played in China's success has started to evolve during the past twenty-two years following the 1997 handover.

At the peak of its influence in 1993 Hong Kong accounted for a staggering 27% of China's entire GDP. However, today that significance has fallen to a mere 2.9% of China's GDP, not because Hong Kong's GDP is shrinking but because cities and economic zones across China have averaged annual GDP growth of 7 to 8% for the past 25 years. Once serving as the "window into China" during the early years of the PRC government, Hong Kong has now fallen prey to the abundant number of direct entry points into China. Shanghai, known as the "Pearl of the Orient" in the 1930s, has essentially re-emerged with its population of 26 million people as the rightful business and economic center of China. There have been other economic success stories as well. Take for example Hong Kong's next door neighbor just across the border in mainland China, the city of Shenzhen. A sleepy city of less than 30,000 residents during the 1970s, today Shenzhen boasts a population of 12.5 million residents and in 2017 its GDP surpassed that of Hong Kong. Guangdong Province boasts a population of 113 million spread over 36 counties. Its top nine urban centers comprise the Greater Bay Area (GBA) which has a total population just under 70 million people (slightly larger than the population of the United Kingdom) (see Fig. 2.9). By 2017 the Greater Bay Area's economy had reached a level of economic magnitude that would place its annual GDP of USD 1.51 trillion at 13th largest in the world just slightly larger than the GDP of Australia (USD 1.38 trillion)! (see Table 2.1).

Other Issues

From a Western perspective it may seem easy to point an accusatory finger at China for the situation that has developed on the streets of Hong Kong in recent weeks. However, one might take a more balanced view if one accounts for the backstop that China has provided to the Hong Kong economy for the past two decades under Chinese rule. Undeniably the economy and infrastructure of Hong Kong under China's watch has remained buoyant and resilient and, in fact, improved. In June 2003, the mainland and Hong Kong penned the Closer Economic Partnership Arrangement (called locally, CEPA) in order to accord special privileges to Hong Kong businesses that chose to invest in the mainland. Creation of "The Leading Group on the Greater Bay Area" in 2018 Chaired by Vice-Premier Han Zheng has demonstrated the continued commitment

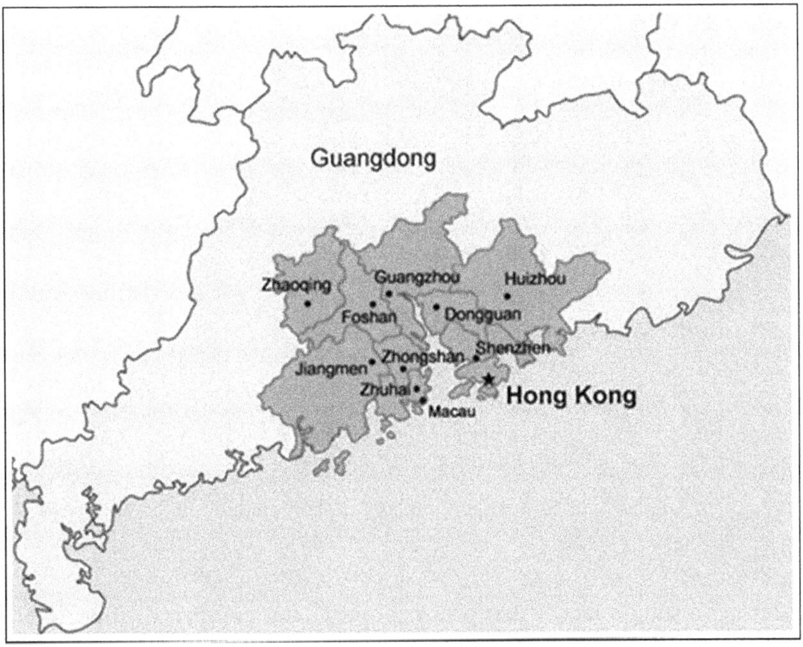

Fig. 2.9 Hong Kong, key economic component of the Greater Bay Area. Hong Kong, Guangdong Province and the GBA: The Bigger Picture of things!

of the Beijing leadership to bring together inter-governmental interaction between local jurisdictions within the GBA region and ensure broad economic initiatives remained on track.

The only exceptions to this uptrend would be the sharp market downturns that occurred during the SARS crisis in 2003 and the steep market correction that occurred in 2008. Otherwise, under Chinese rule Hong Kong's subway and transit system has expanded and become one of the most modern and extensive in the world. It moves over 90% of the Hong Kong population of 7.3 million around every day with remarkable efficiency. Sanitation standards are much higher today than under colonial rule and China has helped to perpetuate and prop up Hong Kong's tourism and retail sector by allowing over 10,000 tourists to cross over the border into Hong Kong each day. What country in Europe or North America would not appreciate so many tourists coming to its major

Table 2.1 Global ranking of the GBA by GDP (vs. other nations)

Rank	*Country*	*GDP USD trillion*
1	United States	19.39
2	China	12.01
3	Japan	4.87
4	Germany	3.68
5	United Kingdom	2.62
6	India	2.61
7	France	2.58
8	Brazil	2.05
9	Italy	1.94
10	Canada	1.65
11	South Korea	1.54
12	Russia	1.53
	GBA	**1.51**
13	Australia	1.38

Source Courtesy of Dr. Michael Enright of the 2022 Foundation study; data from IMF, World Economic Outlook Database (2018)

cities? The simple fact is that today Hong Kong, compared to pre-1997, is bigger, better, faster, cleaner, and more cosmopolitan than it ever was.

However, on the blame side, one cannot also cast a blind side to the imbalances that have also become a by-product of Hong Kong's astonishing success and prioritizing economic activity above all other goals. The imbalances fall into three broad categories:

Side Effects of an Obvious Housing Shortage

Housing prices in Hong Kong have soared over the past decade by 242% while salaries (particularly for young people entering the work force) have increased only slightly more than 12%. Today the average home in Hong Kong is 900 square feet and sells for USD 1.2 million. Factor in as well the world's 3rd highest population density with Hong Kong averaging over 4000 people per square mile (compared to 87 people/square mile in the United States).[3] Simply put, Hong Kong is one of the most expensive

[3] In 2018 Hong Kong ranked 3rd in the world in population density with 7096/sq km following Singapore ranked 2nd (7953/sq km and Macao ranked number 1 (20,778/sq km. To convert to sq mi divide by 1.609 (Source: World Data Atlas 2019).

cities in the world to live in and the quality of housing has not kept pace with Hong Kong's soaring economic success.

The Growing Gap Between the Rich and Poor

Hong Kong offers a contrast of distinctions. In a recent Boston Consulting Group Report on the highest density of millionaires globally, Hong Kong ranked 4th (ahead of both the UK and United States) with 8.6% of all households possessing investible assets exceeding USD 1 million. This result has been achieved despite the fact that its manufacturing sector has essentially moved offshore (mostly to mainland China). By 1997 the Hong Kong economy had shifted from the manufacturing economy of the 1960s and 1970s to a service economy with service industries comprising 85% of its GDP. This trend has continued uninterrupted in the new millennium and service industries reached 92% of GDP by 2016 with financial services, trade-related services, and tourism accounting for nearly 57% of GDP.

However, despite its booming macro-economic figures, enormous disparity of wealth in Hong Kong has been highlighted recently in a study by Oxfam that noted the gap between the rich and the poor in Hong Kong had widened significantly in recent years and was at its highest in 45 years. At current levels, the gap between rich and poor is significantly worse than the gap in the United States or Western Europe. The purchasing power of minimum wage in Hong Kong is worse today than it was 8 years ago. It is estimated that 1 out of 4 youth live below the poverty line—perhaps an explanation of why we see so many young students clad in black shirts in the recent street protests in China. Property price escalation stands out as the most pervasive factor influencing the distribution of wealth issues now facing Hong Kong.

The Need for Educational Reform

Education reform is a hot topic in modern day Hong Kong. For reasons of simplicity, let's take one slither of the educational issue and describe the language policies of schools in Hong Kong. Hong Kongers speak the Cantonese dialect, a dialect common in areas of southern China and, in fact, the same dialect as the early Chinese migrants to the U.S. who built the trans-continental railroad. Under British Colonial rule, both English and Cantonese were the key languages of learning in Hong Kong schools. By contrast language policy in mainland China since 1949 has required that Mandarin (originally a northern dialect) become the language of learning taught in the schools all across China. China has over a dozen major dialects and scores of sub-dialects spread across its 34 provincial level administrative zones (see Fig. 1.3). By adopting Mandarin as the national language of China in 1949 Beijing was seeking to further unify the population and also address widespread illiteracy. Literacy rate in China, hovering just below 20% during World War II has today increased dramatically reaching a level above 90%. (Note: Mandarin is also the dialect of Chinese that is universally taught to language students around the world at most universities in Europe and North America.)

Since Hong Kong's retrocession back to China in 1997, Mandarin has been flourishing as a dialect among Hong Kong residents. However, under the "One Countries, Two Systems" promised to Hong Kongers by the 1997 "Basic Law" handover accords, Cantonese dialect has been allowed to remain the dialect of learning in most Hong Kong public schools. It should be noted that Cantonese speakers and Mandarin speakers essentially read the same chinese character text. However, an innocent bystander listening to the same passage being recited by both Cantonese or Mandarin speakers would be astonished listening to such passage. They sound like two distinctively different languages. Chinese is essentially a tonal language. Mandarin, the national dialect, has four tones. Cantonese has 7 tones. I have known cases where friends from Beijing find it easier to speak English with people from Hong Kong than trying to speak Mandarin or Cantonese. Watching the nightly news in America about the Hong Kong protests, one might think the difference in dialect spoken in Beijing and Hong Kong is like a New Yorker speaking to someone from New Orleans. However, it is more akin to someone from Copenhagen trying to speak to someone from Sicily—from a narrow listening comprehension perspective, they are two very different languages.

The language policy in Hong Kong implemented by the government allows an element of autonomy to be preserved in Hong Kong culture and daily life. However, one could make the argument that, in the new economy and age of globalism, requiring Mandarin dialect to be the dialect of learning in Hong Kong (like what is practiced in Singapore schools)[4] might actually prepare young Hong Kongers more readily for

[4] Mandarin Chinese was not widely spoken in Singapore in the 1960s when Singapore broke off from the Malaysian Federation and became a sovereign nation despite the population being 70% ethnically Chinese. A series of educational reforms resulted in an

the job market than the current language policy. At present, the sense of local Cantonese pride and self-determination in Hong Kong which has been honored to date by Beijing's in adherence to "One country, two systems" stands in the way of such reform. If a dramatic change in medium of language learning is to occur, Hong Kongers themselves must make the tough decision to embrace it.

Beyond language policy there are other contentious educational issues in Hong Kong schools too complex to cover within the confines of this study. However, the issue of language policy and the flexibility over use of Cantonese dialect in schools continues to perpetuate Hong Kong's uniqueness. Whereas allowing teaching in Cantonese ensures Hong Kong retains its uniqueness, the flip side of the coin requires self-reflection and may foster the question "would implementing a language policy in Hong Kong schools that requires both Mandarin and English guarantee that young Hong Kongers can more readily compete for jobs in the global marketplace?" Within the Asia-Pacific region are young Hong Kongers able to compete in job markets throughout Asia on equal standing with other Chinese from the mainland, Taiwan, Malaysia, and Singapore who have been educated in Mandarin in their schools since early childhood? What policy adjustment would be suitable for creating a path forward that will promote not only career opportunities for youth but also greater unity and assimilation into China?

In summary, there is the risk of great miscalculation and misunderstanding of unfolding events in Hong Kong by Western media and observers. Radical elements within the students (sometimes waving British and American flags) have sought to turn the mass protests into a movement about freedom and democracy. Meanwhile, to many Chinese both in Hong Kong and in China, there is a certain disdain for seeing British and American flags on territory that rightfully belongs to China. (Note: Most Americans would likewise not be happy seeing a Chinese flag being flown in Hawaii or downtown of a major U.S. city.) Also, the British ruled Hong Kong for 150 years and never introduced universal suffrage as a means for selecting the leader of Hong Kong. Is Beijing now just 22 years since 1997 really less democratic than London was for 146 years? Clearly the U.S. National Guard would have been called out long ago if

official bi-lingual language policy by 1980. A majority of young Singaporeans (even many from Indian and Malay ethnic background) selected Mandarin as 2nd language to study in their school system along with English which is required.

street protests of this magnitude and violence had occurred in a U.S. major city. Beijing so far has exercised enormous restraint by not calling out their military as they know to do so would risk global condemnation (even though the British did it in the 1960s).

CHAPTER 3

Hong Kong's Role in the Sino-U.S. Trade War: Caught Between the Crosshairs

Abstract This chapter analyses the oft misunderstood aspects of the Sino-U.S. trade relationship. It highlights the dangerous historical precedent of restricting free trade in the 1930s wrought by the U.S. Congressional passage of the Smoot-Hawley Act (1930). A case is made for the Theory of Comparative Advantage by Nineteenth Century English statesman David Ricardo. Opportunities for continuing global growth or descending into global chaos is the stark choice ahead of us depending upon the willingness of the U.S. and China to work through trade differences.

Keywords Hong Kong Human Rights and Democracy Act (HKHRDA) · Trade deficit · Balance of payments · Smoot-Hawley Act (1930) · Theory of Comparative Advantage by Ricardo

B. VonCannon, *Status Anxiety*,
https://doi.org/10.1007/978-981-15-7028-5_3

However, the story of the success that many American companies have made in recent years in the China market deserves to be told. Take the example of General Motors. It has increased sales of General Motors automobiles in China by four times in the past decade. It sold four million GM cars in the China market in 2015, more than it sold on its home continent in North America (Fig. 3.1).

In addition, let's take the Chinese mobile phone market. Forty years ago fixed line telephones were so rare in China in the early reformist years under Deng Xiao Ping in the late 70s and early 80s that many American companies would place phone calls to Beijing at the beginning of the day and usually leave the long distance phone line open most of the day. This was because it was so difficult to get a foreign phone call through to China given the extremely limited number of fixed lines. Fast forward to the Twenty-First Century and China has skipped a generation of fixed line deployments and become the world's largest mobile phone market.

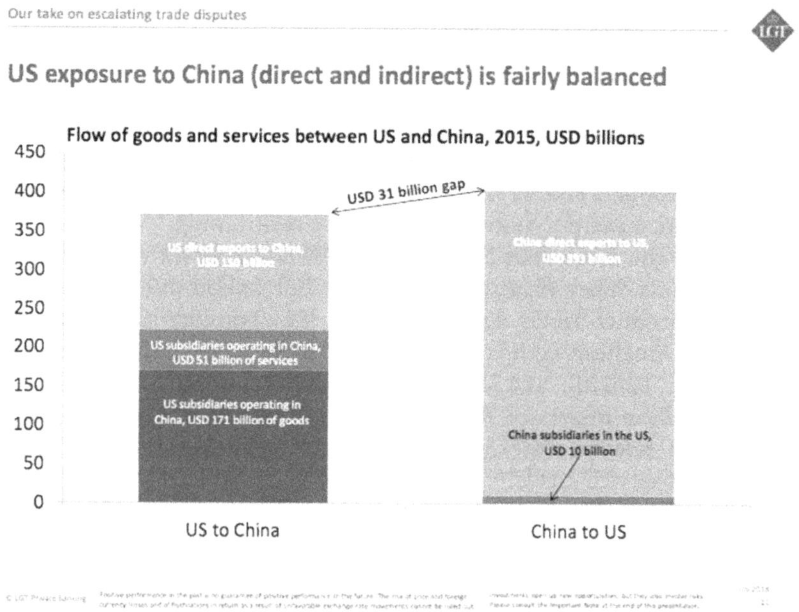

Fig. 3.1 Flow of goods and services between US and China (*Source* Deutsche Bank, LGT, March 2018)

The U.S. brand, Apple, has enjoyed outstanding success in the Chinese domestic market and sales revenue in 2016 exceeded USD 45 billion. This is a staggering figure when compared to China's exports of cell phones to the U.S. market which totaled only about USD 200 million during the same year. USD 45 billion to USD 200 million! In Trumpian terms "who's winning?".

To be balanced in one's discussion of the trade issue with China, one must candidly admit that there are trading practices by both the U.S. and China that are still needing review. China must continue to strengthen enforcement of Intellectual Property Rights (IPR) within China to both enable fair litigation against IPR abusers as well as change the existing perspective held in the United States and Europe that China does not respect IPR.[1]

China has a legacy of benefitting from its low starting base economically in trade negotiations undertaken with the West in the 1970s and early 80s as it began to emerge from the disastrous Maoist economic policies of the previous two decades. However, since its entry into the WTO in December 2001 China has been obliged to adopt the trading practices of more modern, developed countries. Incumbent with its newly minted WTO membership, China has increasingly opened its economy to goods and services and lowered import duties and "hidden barriers" to free trade. There are still obstacles to be overcome and multi-lateral trade negotiations and dialogue are essential to resolving these issues. The role of the WTO, controversial to many, still remains the "least bad" forum for ironing out trade disputes when certain differences in perspective cannot be resolved by the countries themselves (Fig. 3.2).

What Are the Implications of Regressing into a World That Limits Free Trade?

One should consider what lessons in history might apply to the current trade tensions between China and the U.S. and the general debate about

[1] In a recent American Chamber of Commerce conference in Guangzhou in 2019 it was suggested in presentations that "perjury," a concept that exists under U.S. legal process is not a federal crime in China of the same magnitude that it is in the U.S. thereby slowing the process in China of arbitrating against IPR infringement. Recent trends in China, however, suggest the government is seeking to invigorate IPR enforcement within Chinese courts.

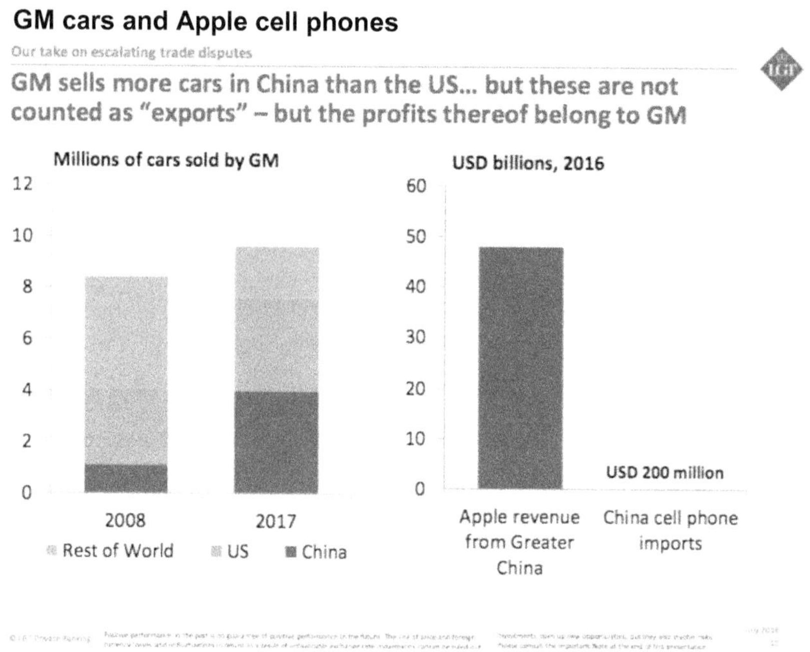

Fig. 3.2 Sales figures for GM cars and Apple cell phones in China (*Source* Deutsche Bank, LGT, March 2018)

global trade. In the 1930s just following the colossal drop in the U.S. Stock market and onset of the Great Depression, two members of U.S. Congress, Senator Reed Smoot of Utah and House Representative Willis Hawley of Oregon, aligned forces to push across U.S. Congressional approval of the Smoot Hawley Act of 1930 thinking that by restricting the flow of goods into the United States it would benefit American citizens and stimulate the U.S. economy. Following the passage of the act import tariffs were raised on over 900 product classifications by an average of 40%.

In the ensuing months following the passage of the Smoot Hawley Act the U.S. stock market continued to plunge. Job unemployment, far from recovering, plunged further. In addition to U.S. actions, retaliatory actions by other governments around the world began to occur. The United Kingdom and France both raised import duties reflexively in order seemingly to protect their markets. Over the course of the coming five years after the passage of Smoot Hawley, global trade plunged by 60% exacerbating an already unstable and chaotic global political and economic landscape. Fascist governments in Germany under Adolf Hitler and in Italy under Benito Mussolini tightened their control on power. In Japan, a military grip on the government further consolidated its power, too (Fig. 3.3).

The immediate net effect of the Smoot Hawley Act was to prolong the Great Depression and lower (not raise) American living standards. The longer term impact, however, is still debated as some historians believe it led to heightened global tensions that eventually led to the outbreak of World War II.

Fig. 3.3 Smoot and Hawley: Well-intentioned but harbingers of a grossly flawed economic policy!

The story of Mssr. Smoot and Hawley did not end well. By as early as 1932, their stunning lack of judgement did them in. Both were defeated in the election of 1932 that swept Franklin D. Roosevelt into power. Smoot and Hawley both returned to their native Utah and Oregon respectively, both dying in obscurity in the same year in 1941 just at the outset of World War II. Their seldom mentioned role in American history hardly belies the harm and wealth destruction that their policies caused.

How Can Educating the American and Chinese Public Be Improved?

An argument that has been lost amidst the shouting in the debates about free trade and globalism is the case for open markets and lowering trade tariffs. The world has benefited enormously over the past 70 years from the series of trade agreements that began with the General Agreement on Tariffs and Trade (GATT) that was signed by 23 nations just after World War II. Fresh on the minds of our leaders both in the United States and in Europe and Asia at that time in 1945 was the catastrophic effect that a breakdown in global trade had played in the events that led to World War II, a war that resulted in over 65 million deaths between the years of 1937 and 1945.

GATT helped to stabilize the global system of trade after World War II. Far from perfect, it at least created a channel for countries to publicly air their differences on perceived or real unfair trade practices. The world of the 1950s was very different from what we experience today. Regrettably an ideological war between the United States and former Soviet Union resulted in a Cold War that essentially divided the world into the two trading blocs, NATO countries aligned with the United States and Warsaw Pact countries mostly of Eastern Europe aligned with the former Soviet Union. Non-aligned countries like India and China also attempted for form alliances as an offset to the NATO/Warsaw Pact rivalry. However, trade was subservient to ideology.

The fall of the Berlin Wall in 1989 ushered in changes of epic proportions. Suddenly the Cold War began to thaw. Ideology which had resulted in decades of distrust, misunderstanding, and misallocation of resources fomenting an arms race, fell by the wayside as countries, particularly in Europe, began to see the benefits of cross border flow of goods and services. The exchange and implementation of new ideas and larger numbers of work visas for both skilled and unskilled labor pools began to flourish. In essence, the world has largely benefitted from the fall of the Berlin Wall. It should be remembered as a shining moment in history when pragmatism overtook ideology.

Shifting the discussion back to the critical need to educate and insulate the public from the growing xenophobia in the Western press, it might be helpful to also cite the arguments for free trade embodied in the writings of Nineteenth Century U.K. economist/statesman David Ricardo who espoused the "Theory of Comparative Advantage." Ricardo was born into the family of a Jewish stockbroker in Portugal who disowned him after he eloped in marriage. Overcoming many odds early in his life young Ricardo made his way to England where he educated himself and would through his own merits prosper in a career in banking and finance. He also eventually entered the U.K. parliament and became a vigorous supporter of free trade. Sadly he died at the young age of 51. However, Ricardo wrote prolifically until his death and his writings have been preserved by historians and economists and had profound impact on the economic policies of many nations, particularly the liberal democracies of the Twentieth Century (Fig. 3.4).

During Ricardo's lifetime the prevailing practice by nations that had dominated world trade for two centuries was "mercantilism." Its proponents sought to foster the idea that a country should conduct trade for the purpose of earning as much hard currency as possible by achieving trade surpluses with its trading partners. Ricardo was an implacable opponent of this way of thinking. He espoused the view that countries should seek industry specialization and free trade. He believed that a country should concentrate its resources vis-à-vis trading partners on industries where it has "comparative advantage" or another way of saying in street language "focus on your strengths." Today the global supply chain that has developed to such a high level of sophistication since the Berlin Wall fell in 1989 is essentially an outgrowth of Ricardian theory.

However, let us digress for more back story on the Sino-U.S. trade relationship. As new solutions are sought to break the deadlock that has developed under the Trump administration, it is worthwhile to note why it is in both nations' best interests to seek a new paradigm in their trading relationship.

First, let's look at mainland China. China has enjoyed soaring economic development since the early 1980s. Annual GDP growth figures provided by the World Bank show China averaging anemic growth during the years of 1960 to 1979—figures hard to accurately depict since the

Fig. 3.4 David Ricardo (1772–1823): Father of the "Theory of Comparative Advantage" or why we shop for baby clothes for $19.95 at Walmart today!

years of the Cultural Revolution (1966–1976) China was in a virtual state of civil war greatly impairing the forces of economic progress. However, following the ascendancy of Deng Xiao-Ping to power in the post-Mao era, China GDP growth soared to new heights averaging annual GDP growth of 9.91% between the years 1979 to 2010. While there has been a general slowing of the economy following the Great Financial Crisis of 2008, China's average annual GDP growth rate since this date has still managed to achieve 5.0–7.0% annually. The macro figures in China, even with a slowing of GDP growth, are hard to dispute as the growth rates are double the rate of the U.S. and Western Europe during roughly the same time period.

When one seeks to know how this staggering growth has occurred, we should not forget that there was a period of Chinese history when the country was economically, socially, and intellectually far ahead of the Western world. Take for example, Fifteenth Century China under the Ming Dynasty which coincidentally is the setting for an enlightening book written by former Royal British naval officer and author, Gavin Menzies entitled "1421: The Year China Discovered America." There were probably more printed books in the Imperial Library in Beijing in the early 1400s than existed in all of Western Europe (which was just emerging from the Dark Ages). The cynical and hypocritical style in which Western trade negotiations have frequently been depicted over the past few years by jaundiced right wing journalists has been grossly off the mark. It has implied that China is a copycat country that only steals technology. Such exaggerations are grossly overstated and often self-serving by those launching the accusations. China's track record on funding research and development (R&D) on the global stage is not insignificant. While the U.S. does actually spend slightly more than China on R&D, USD 553 billion to USD 475 billion or 2.84% of GDP and 1.97% of GDP respectively, the two countries along with Japan lead the world in R&D.[2] In the space of theft of technology in today's competitive world, no one country is guilty. It is neither a Chinese nor a U.S. phenomenon. There would be a long list of companies from many continents under many country flags if ever there was an unbiased master list of "who dunnit?" compiled? Lest we forget that throughout world history China has also enjoyed their share of technological breakthroughs and inventions dating back to Yellow Emperor Lei Zu and the invention of silk weaving around 3000 B.C. Paper was first used by the Chinese in 100 B.C. during the Han Dynasty, and gunpowder (yes, the most revolutionary military technology of its time) was first used by the Chinese in the Ninth Century under the Tang Dynasty.

[2] Japan actually leads the world in percentage of GDP allocated to R&D but ranked third in nominal amount (USD 186 billion). Germany (USD 116 billion) and South Korea (USD 99 billion) ranked 4th and 5th globally. Source: US News and World Report (November 9, 2018).

While we marvel at the development of China during the past 30 years we should also caution that that such extraordinary economic development during such a brief period of time has come with a price tag as well. China still faces enormous domestic challenges today. These challenges are markedly different from the challenges that existed in the past century when providing basics for survival (food, shelter, and housing) were lacking for a large swath of Chinese society. Take for example China's enormous population of 1.3 billion which is roughly four times the population of the United States. One would think that a population of that size would never suffer from an insufficient labor force. However, after 30 years of a one-child policy, China now has become a ticking time bomb in its demographic structure. The labor force in China actually began to shrink for the first time in 2011 and has now fallen for seven consecutive years.[3] Suddenly the absence of the traditional Chinese family which relied on large numbers for children to collectively take care of their parents as they aged, is now the cause of tremendous social strain. Poverty among people aged 65 or older is a serious social problem today in China which authorities openly acknowledge and are trying to correct. The divorce rate in China, something taboo and unmentionable in past decades, has also spiked up significantly just like in many Western countries. This has further exacerbated the problem of who should bear the responsibility of taking care of the elderly.

Traditional light industry jobs have been fleeing China at a brisk rate. Just ask a factory owner in China! They will lament the soaring cost of labor as being a factor that is driving China further away from its traditional role as being an "export driven economy." It has propelled forward the transformation process of China increasingly becoming a "domestic driven economy." No industry is pre-ordained to stay in a given country or location indefinitely. Factories in light industry product areas like footwear, textiles, and luggage have been relocating to lower labor cost countries like Vietnam, Cambodia, Indonesia, and Bangladesh at a staggering rate just like the exodus of textile factories out of New England in the United States into rural areas of North and South Carolina in the 1940s and 50s. Today in Beijing economic planners and authorities may be reluctant to see the cheap, labor jobs depart China and wish such job attrition could occur at a slower rate. However, they see it as an

[3] Source: China's National Bureau of Statistics (2018).

inevitable progression and sign of economic transition. They would like lost jobs to be replaced by jobs that produce higher value-added products and services. Just over a decade ago, China was captive to America's trade demands with over 30% of its exports going to the U.S. market. Today that figure has fallen below 20%. It is still significant, but China today can afford to stand up to what it perceives as being unreasonable trade demands or bullying trade negotiation tactics.

Take also the example of the environment in China. Unbridled economic development has resulted in China facing unprecedented air and water pollution problems in its major cities. A natural environment analysis conducted by Tsinghua University and the Asian Development Bank in 2013 revealed that China had 7 out of 10 of the most polluted cities in the world. When one adopts a top-down, command style model for achieving economic growth, the risk is it rides roughshod over all other secondary development goals in society including those that encroach upon environmental protection and general health and lifestyle. Leadership in Beijing is aware of these side effects and have declared more and more urban zones to be manufacturing free. It is one further bit of evidence why the status quo (not only unacceptable in the United States) is also considered unsustainable and unacceptable by a large swathe of the Chinese population as well.

A glance at micro economic factors are also helpful to our analysis. Just like the average American, the typical Chinese citizen lives and saves and consumes. A very impressive statistic about Chinese families is their average savings rate which is approximately 20% and significantly higher than the average savings rates documented in many western countries. The turbulence in Chinese history over the past 100 years has certainly been a factor driving this statistic as the quote "keep your money for a rainy day" has certainly been a wise thing to do if one has experienced and endured the many wars and natural disasters (e.g. earthquakes, floods, droughts) that have afflicted China during the past two centuries. However, other cultural practices and lifestyle choices in China encourage Chinese from an early age to save money after each pay check. Most young Chinese live in the family home until they marry, a custom that also contributes in a positive way to the high savings rate. Chinese consumers also have become the world leader in e-commerce. It is estimated in 2018 that close to 30% of retail transactions taking place in China are done online (compared to 18% in the United States). China has become almost 50% of the global e-commerce market while the U.S. is 2nd with approximately 20% of the market. Hand-in-hand with e-commerce goes the development of online payment systems, another industry in which China leads the world. Chinese do much of their consumer purchasing largely through online payment systems (e.g. Alipay, Union Pay, We Chat Pay) that are more sophisticated than what exists in almost every country in the West.

The trade issue, if taken from the perspective of the United States, provides further evidence why the status quo in Sino-U.S. global trade cannot be maintained. While nobody disputes the fact that the United States remains the global leader in GDP growth and military prowess, those areas of invincibility cannot be assumed ad infinitum. Average American families continue to nurse wounds suffered during the Global financial Crisis of 2008. Real median wage levels for U.S. workers are up only 10% higher than they were in 1973. Per capital savings rates in the U.S. were in the 6% range during the last three decades of the Twentieth Century. However, they have fallen to 3% per capita in 2018, a stark difference compared to China's impressive 20% per capita savings rate. It highlights the structural differences in the economy of China and that of the United States.

Viewed from 30,000 feet, the U.S. economy still enjoys enormous advantages over the Chinese economy. The U.S. accounts for 21% of global annual GDP compared to a global total of 15% for China (see Fig. 3.5). The U.S. accounts for 33% of global household income while China stands at under 15%. However, these macro figures mask the issues of "income gap" (i.e. the gap of rich vs. poor) which has become a global phenomenon. Home ownership in China today stands at 84% while in the United States the figure has fallen to approximately 63%. The growth trends favor China's ascent as an economic power which the West must come to terms with. With its annual GDP growth rates at double those of the United States, the size of the Chinese economy could potentially overtake the U.S. economy within the coming decade. U.S. productivity rates averaged 3.2% from 1987 to 2016. In the past five years, U.S. productivity has fallen to an anemic 0.5%.

In summary, the limits of China's powerful export driven economy have been reached. European and U.S. economies with their slowing birth rates and sluggish savings rates have "tapped out" and reached maximum import market value for China. It is one of the reasons that China has launched aggressively the "One Belt, One Road" (BRI) initiative as well as the Asian Infrastructure and Investment Bank (AIIB) in

近期GDP排名前十的经济体

Lists

Per the International Monetary Fund (2017)[17]			Per the World Bank (2017)[21]			Per the United Nations (2016)[22][23]		
Rank	Country	GDP (US$million)	Rank	Country	GDP (US$million)	Rank	Country	GDP (US$million)
	World[20]	**79,865,481**		*World*	**80,683,787**		*World*[25]	**75,648,448**
1	United States	19,390,600	1	United States	19,390,604	1	United States	18,624,475
2	China[n 1]	12,014,610		*European Union*[24]	17,277,698	2	China[n 4]	11,218,281
3	Japan	4,872,135	2	China[n 4]	12,237,700	3	Japan	4,936,211
4	Germany	3,684,816	3	Japan	4,872,137	4	Germany	3,477,796
5	United Kingdom	2,624,529	4	Germany	3,677,439	5	United Kingdom	2,647,898
6	India	2,611,012	5	United Kingdom	2,622,434	6	France	2,465,453
7	France	2,583,560	6	India	2,597,491	7	India	2,259,642
8	Brazil	2,054,969	7	France	2,582,501	8	Italy	1,858,913
9	Italy	1,937,894	8	Brazil	2,055,506	9	Brazil	1,795,925
10	Canada	1,652,412	9	Italy	1,934,798	10	Canada	1,529,760

Fig. 3.5 Recent ranking of top ten GDP economies (by nominal GDP) (*Source* IMF [2018], World Bank [2018], and United Nations [2018])

2016. They need new export markets. Beyond the political embarrassment that exorbitant trade surplus figures now represent when China sits down to the negotiating table with its European and American trading partners, at home China must bring higher quality of life standards to its populace with is newfound wealth. China's most recent Communist Party Plenum in 2019 announced a commitment to improve the quality of life of its people. They know delivering economic success without it having a trickle-down effect to the average family represents an unsustainable path for the Beijing leadership. China's economic model and GDP growth the past 30 years has been overly dependent on export growth and public investment into infrastructure as an elixir for economic robustness. Beijing authorities are aware of this unsustainable trend. In most developed economies in North America and Western Europe consumer activity accounts for approximately 65% of annual GDP growth. In China, this figure has stayed below 35% much of the past 30 years and has only started to climb in recent years with Beijing's concerted efforts to induce "domestic demand." Time will tell if this transition can be achieved.

The U.S. side of the argument has already begun. The election of Donald Trump, for better or for worse, signified the desire for change by the American middle class. Certainly, a vigorous exchange between the U.S. and China and Europe on bi-lateral trade issues was to be expected. What is enigmatic is the controversial manner in which the Trump White House has conducted the negotiations. The Trump Administration rhetoric, while addressing the need to cut or eliminate the trade deficit with China as the be-all, end-all argument, has failed to mention that China itself has periodically suffered trade deficits with other countries.[4] U.S. companies and service providers do maintain a "surplus" with China in the service sector and, as noted above, this helps to mitigate the deficits incurred in product exported to the United States. The import of lower cost (particularly) consumer items have traditionally helped keep U.S. inflation figures down which is a benefit to all American consumers. A 3rd quarter 2019 report by J. P. Morgan warned that additional tariffs announced to be implemented later in the year could raise annual costs to U.S. families by USD 900 per family. When the U.S. economy has its lowest unemployment figures in 50 years at approximately 3.6%,[5] and is almost reaching full employment, the accusation that China is stealing jobs from the U.S. does not reflect an entirely true scenario.

Other trade figures and the receipt of losses to American companies has become longer and more varied. The promise of USD 50 billion in agriculture buys by China announced by the Trump administration (to put it mildly) are overblown. In the two years prior to the disruptive trade policies launched by the White House, the U.S. agricultural business community racked up USD 49 billion in sales to China. However, at the outset of 2020 figures showed year-on-year bankruptcies in the U.S. agribusiness sector up 20% owing primarily to retaliatory tariffs against US agriculture products resurrected by China. Figures released by UBS AG at the of end 3rd quarter 2019 showed a 19% drop in export volume to China from the Port of Los Angeles, the largest port in the United States, and costing US companies sales estimated at USD 19 billion. The actual flow of trade also paints a very different set of figures in other industries beyond agriculture. Before the trade war started, U.S. liquified natural gas sales to China accounted for 4.3% of Chinese imports and 16% of US. LNG exports. By late summer in 2019 China had announced expanding

[4] China incurred a trade deficit in US Dollars in 2018 with these major trading partners: Taiwan (128 bln), S Korea (95 bln), Australia (57 bln), Brazil (43 bln), Switzerland (34 bln), Japan (33 bln), Germany (28 bln), and Saudi Arabia (28 bln) (Source: Worldstop exports.com).

[5] U.S. unemployment figures released by the U.S. Bureau of Labor Statistics in October 2019 showed 3.6% unemployment rate, the lowest unemployment figures in 50 years.

its LNG relationships with Qatar and Australia and, meanwhile, reducing LNG imports from the U.S. to 1% of Chinese imports. The same story is echoed in crude oil exports to China from the U.S. They had fallen from 20% of total U.S. crude oil exports to 1% by late 3rd quarter 2019. The effect of the signing of the Phase 1 trade agreement between the U.S. and China in January 2020 has at least revived hope that a roadmap to a more balanced trade relationship between the world's two great economic powers can be developed over time. The practical effect of this Phase 1 announcement was that it represents a truce on the implementation of more trade tariffs and gives both sides some face-saving positions to relish before the upcoming US presidential election in November 2020.

Following the slowing of Chinese economy in 4th quarter 2019, the opening weeks of 2020 began with another crisis of even larger proportions looming on the horizon with the outbreak of the coronavirus (COVID-19) in the centrally located Chinese city of Wuhan in Hubei Province. Chinese authorities were criticized initially for the slowness in acknowledging the outbreak of this deadly virus. However, by early January the extent of the outbreak of the virus and its deadliness as well as its highly contagious nature was disclosed and brought forth to the World Health Organization (WHO) in Geneva. The rockiness of the U.S.-China trade relationship has sporadically spilled over into the cooperative talks within the WHO with U.S. and other country delegates squabbling over the wording of joint communiques. Longer term it is hoped that collaboration will win over ideology when it comes to U.S. and China joint efforts to control the spread of Covid-19 and the efforts underway to develop a vaccine that can cure this serious threat to humanity. Hopes for such global cooperation and initiatives in the sphere of healthcare and biotech to fight spread of infectious diseases received another setback in early April 2020 when the Trump White House announced it was suspending USD 500 million in annual funding for the WHO in Geneva. This rash act came just as the President's popularity was plunging and he was reeling from accusations by opposition lawmakers and health experts over his mishandling of the Covid-19 pandemic in the United States.

Beyond the complex issues surrounding the U.S.-China trade relationship and who commands the moral high ground, the prevailing sentiment within Hong Kong corporate offices is most emphatically "please leave the Hong Kong protests alone and do not mix it up in the U.S.-China trade negotiations." Most local and expatriate executives in Hong Kong deplored the visit by U.S. Senators Ted Cruz (R-Texas) and Josh Hawley

(R-Missouri) in October 2019 in order to appear at a rally with some of the black shirt protestors and making the assertion that demonstrators had acted non-violently in the previous five months of protests. Hong Kong Chief Executive Carrie Lam cancelled a meeting with Cruz and Hawley after they scheduled a meeting with protestors without any prior consultation. In addition, their visit was lambasted in the leading Hong Kong newspaper, the "South China Morning Post," and particularly Cruz's role to which the paper's article labeled Cruz as being "utterly clueless"[6] and called him "just about the worst specimen of American politicians" and seeking "an opening with the Hong Kong riots to be exploited for Washington's new cold war against China." One of Cruz's campaign backers in Texas, hedge fund manager, Kyle Bass, bantered in mid-2019 that the protests would bring down the Hong Kong dollar on global currency markets which to date seems at odds with market fundamentals.[7] In fairness to Cruz and Hawley they did make overtures to the protestors to adopt non-violent means when voicing their opposition to government policies. However, the overall impression left by the Cruz-Hawley visit was that it was a public relations disaster and sadly appearing to be evidence of U.S. interference into local politics for a U.S. domestic agenda rather than truly playing a helpful role to act as an intermediary between two opposing sides.

[6] Kindly refer to coverage of Cruz and Hawley visit in October 14, 2019 edition of *South China Morning Post*.

[7] The HK Dollar/US Dollar exchange rate has been pegged between 7.75 and 7.85 to 1 since 1983 by the "linked exchange rate system (LERS)" adopted by the Hong Kong Monetary Authority (HKMA). The LERS policy is backstopped by the HKMA's massive Exchange Fund which is estimated at over USD 511 billion. HK's foreign currency reserves exceed that of many countries (Source: *South China Morning Post*, November 9, 2019).

CHAPTER 4

The Tale of Two Cities: Hong Kong and Shenzhen

Abstract This chapter describes the symbiotic nature of the relationship between Hong Kong and Shenzhen since the formation of China's Special Economic Zones (SEZs) in the early 1980s under the reformist leadership of paramount Chinese leader Deng Xiao-Ping. It underlines the critical balance that must be maintained between harnessing the enormous economic growth potential for Hong Kong and Shenzhen and the Greater Bay alliance which must be juggled with the priority of addressing Hong Kong's growing gap between rich and poor, its housing crisis, and mending the cultural differences between Hong Kong and the mainland.

Keywords Hong Kong pro-democracy movement's five demands · Hong Kong's lost generation · Hong Kong's housing crisis · Cities of the Greater Bay Area (GBA)

B. VonCannon, *Status Anxiety*,
https://doi.org/10.1007/978-981-15-7028-5_4

Crisis in the Kingdom of Yue[1]—Hong Kong's retarded entry into the GBA!

One of the causes of great concern over the Hong Kong protests has been the lack of practical demands coming from the protesters that could make an immediate measurable difference to solve the underlying social problems in Hong Kong. The current demands from the protesters lack specifics that the Hong Kong government could reasonably adopt as a road map and allow for face-saving on both sides. A full six months after the protests started there had been no actionable demand coming from the protesters related to the housing crisis. There had been no mention of the obvious growing gap between rich and poor nor a specifically proposed measure to address it. The slogans "Five demands, not one less" and an oft seen graffiti plastered around areas of the city, "If we burn, you burn with us" seemed so strident as to suggest an intention by the protestors to overthrow the government. This seems a gigantic leap beyond the intensity of the protests that brought massive numbers

[1] Yue (or Yu Yue) was a state in ancient China that existed during the first millennium B.C. It was the area of southern Yue (Yuehai region) that includes part of today's Guangdong Province. Even today when a Chinese asks another in Mandarin "do you speak Cantonese?" they literally say "do you speak the language of Yue?".

into the streets of Hong Kong in 2003 over the planned enactment of Article 23[2] and again during the 79 days Occupy Central and the Umbrella Movement in 2014.[3] As 2019 came to a close it was obvious that much dialogue is needed to overcome the polarization that had set in and festered during the second half of the year.

A Leaderless Protest? What Is the Way Out of the Crisis?

This has been the most difficult aspect of containing this crisis. While the protesters do have speakers at rallies that they have staged, they are seemingly a leaderless movement or broadly splintered into small protests cells. They remain agile and well-organized in protest. They adhere to a philosophy of protest "to act like water" and remain unpredictable when and where they will strike next to protest in Hong Kong districts. However, there is a lack of discipline over who speaks for all protestors and who controls their ability to accept and honor compromises that might actually lead to meaningful negotiations that could end the violence. As a result, the "Five demands, not one less" slogan of the protesters have been really difficult to be accepted by government authorities. Let us take a brief look at each of the five demands:

i. Demand #1—Full withdrawal of the extradition bill

The initial protests which started in June 2019 were the result of this very issue and the strong broad-based support to overturn it. Over a half

[2] On July 1st 2003 over 500,000 Hong Kong residents flooded the streets in protest to voice anger against the Hong Kong SAR government's plan to enact Article 23 of the Basic Law which states that the Hong Kong SAR government "shall enact laws on its own to prohibit any act of treason, secession, sedition, subversion against the Central People's government, or theft of state secrets, to prohibit foreign political organizations or bodies from establishing ties with foreign political organizations or bodies." The bill was withdrawn and shelved indefinitely after it became apparent that it would not meet with approval from the HK Legislative Council.

[3] A series of sit-in street protests began in September 2014 and resulted in protesters occupying major roads in Hong Kong's Central District for 79 days lasting until December 15. The key demand of the protestors was universal suffrage in the elections for Hong Kong Chief Executive. However, the Hong Kong government has not acquiesced to the demand to allow universal suffrage and given no specific date for its implementation.

a million Hong Kong residents turned out in the streets in June mostly in a peaceful manner to oppose this resolution. However, the Hong Kong government eventually backed away from this issue and officially withdrew the bill in October 2019. Meanwhile, radical elements using the ignition provided by the extradition issue have morphed the protest into a broader based pro-democracy movement (with fringe elements of the protestors seeking Hong Kong independence or the outright overthrow of the Hong Kong SAR government).

ii. Demand #2—An independent inquiry into alleged police brutality

Have there been over the past several months instances of "police brutality?" Probably. Have there been examples of protestors bullying Hong Kong residents, committing wanton acts of vandalism against public transport and infrastructure, and conducting brutal forms of harassment not only against police but also against their spouses and children? Most definitely yes! If these events had occurred in any major American city, the National Guard would have been called out immediately. However, through the end of 2019 the 6000 PLA military units from China who are stationed in Hong Kong have stayed with their military gear in their barracks except for an instance on one weekend in November 2019. After a weekend of intense riots on one major university campus[4] causing extensive damage, units of the PLA emerged from their local Hong Kong barracks in gym clothes and sneakers to assist as part of a goodwill effort to clean-up one of the nearby campuses. The alleged 12,000 special PLA units on stand-by just across the border in Shenzhen have been held in check by the Beijing government as well. There are an estimated 100,000 additional PLA troops stationed within the southern Chinese geographical perimeter. Strictly from a military point of view, the street protests in Hong Kong could be solved by Chinese military action within 1–2 days. However, the Beijing government is savvy enough to know the potential repercussions that might erupt globally should such a military intervention occur. No matter how justified it might seem to use PLA units to shore up deteriorating public safety and looting in Hong Kong, it would likely be a PR disaster for China globally and they know

[4] Chinese University of Hong Kong (CUHK) campus in Shatin, New Territories was the scene of intense violence using firebombs on 12–13 November 2019. Members of the public and units of the PLA gathered after the riots to help clean up the campus.

it. Taking such action just at a time when China's diplomatic reputation worldwide has actually been rising seems unwise. Within the Asia-Pacific region China has been increasingly viewed as conducting a more stable foreign policy than the erratic foreign policy gestures and inconsistencies of the Trump White House in Washington. China is on a roll. Why put it to risk over Hong Kong?

iii. Demand #3—Retracting the classification of protesters as "rioters"

As 2019 was coming to a close the number of protestors arrested had eclipsed 6000 since the unrest began in early June with an estimated 25% being below the age of 18. Many of those arrested (particularly the minors) have merely been ticketed and given a warning and then released by courts leaving open potential for future prosecution or juvenile corrective action. In most countries a level of violence and vandalism like what has been witnessed in Hong Kong in the second half of 2019 would merit the radical elements of the protestors worthy of the terminology "domestic terrorists" rather than "rioters." Hong Kong Police discovered in the final weeks of 2019 at least two attempts at planning to use improvised explosive devices. In one instance, the culprits included a school teacher and the school's electrician who were in the process of assembling the device presumably with the intention to detonate and harm law enforcement or government authorities. There were isolated interceptions of hand guns being found among protestors. In one instance in December 2019 a 19 year old had obtained an AR-15 assault rifle with over 200 rounds. Attrition rates among the more radical wing of the protestors has increased as several hundred of them have been detained and not released. Under Hong Kong law, "participation in unlawful illegal assembly" is a violation that dates from the colonial period and it carries potentially a prison sentence up to 10 years.[5] Needless to say, the Hong Kong government is not likely to acquiesce to this protester demand anytime soon.

[5] The current Public Order Ordinance was passed by the British colonial government during and in the aftermath of the Hong Kong 1967 riots in order to give the Hong Kong police the authority to arrest rioters.

iv. Demand #4—Amnesty for arrested protestors

Had the level of violence by the protesters followed a more non-violent track resembling the methods of Mahatma Gandhi in India in the 1940s or the civil rights protests led by Dr. Martin Luther King in the U.S. in the 1960s, the discussion of amnesty might be on everyone's lips. However, average Hong Kongers who might have sympathy for the students' cause, have become aghast at the intensity and senselessness of the violence. The protesters' methods have been reminiscent of scenes from a "Hunger Games" style movie. The methods have been intent on disrupting and systematically destroying Hong Kong's infrastructure. Hong Kong boasts having one of the most modern and sophisticated mass transit systems in the world—in fact, copied by urban planners in many other cities in Asia. However, the protesters have seen fit to date to torch and immobilize over two-thirds of Hong Kong's 151 Mass Transit Rail (MTR) stations since the protests began. In addition, angry mobs led by the protesters have targeted mainland Chinese bank branches and retail outlets and restaurants and destroyed malls just before the start of the Christmas holiday season. Many residents of Hong Kong, even those who are sympathetic to the students' cause, consider these violent acts akin to "terrorism" and to be too extreme. They go far beyond civil disobedience.

v. Demand #5—Universal suffrage for both the Legislative Council and the Chief Executive

This is among the most insistent demands of the protestors. Currently the Hong Kong Chief Executive is elected by a body of 1200 delegates who are mostly selected and endorsed by a system over which the Beijing government has some direct control. There is no way to sugarcoat this fact. The current model of selection is not based on the concept of universal suffrage. However, it would not be untruthful to say it is no less autocratic than how the appointment of the Colonial Governor was conducted during the British colonial period from 1842 to 1997.

This demand will likely not be realized in the foreseeable future despite past acknowledgements by the SAR government that working toward universal suffrage could be considered in the future.[6] Hong Kong's Legislative Council (aka Legco) consists of 70 seats. Currently 30 seats are elected from geographical districts across Hong Kong territory. The remaining 40 seats are considered "special (business) constituencies." Opponents of this structure consider the real estate lobby to have too much influence over the Hong Kong government's legislative body.

On November 24 of this past year District Council elections were held on and resulted in over 60% of Hong Kong voters supporting the pro-democracy leaning candidates and, in fact, capturing 70% of the District Council seats. District Councils really exercise no significant authority in Hong Kong. They merely supervise local district parks, libraries, and bus routes. Laws can only be introduced and passed by the Legislative Council in concert with the Chief Executive. However, the District Council elections were viewed by many as a de facto referendum on the government's current policies and effectiveness at handling of the protests. It clearly has served as a wake-up call for the government to listen more carefully to the people of Hong Kong. It will be a sure bet that efforts will likely intensify to reduce the powerful influence of the real estate lobby within the current government. There can be no doubt that the large cross-section of Hong Kong residents yearn for a government which governs in a more inclusive style.

The Lost Generation

Many executives in the business community here consider the youth of Hong Kong today born after 1997 to be members of a lost generation. They lament the fact that most of the kids exhibit traits that are completely at odds with previous generations of Hong Kongers. The traditional view of the city embraced by the mid-career aged residents of Hong Kong is that it is the one place on earth where one can get ahead in life if one is industrious and determined. This spirit is anchored into the Hong Kong ethos by the longstanding tax policies of the Hong

[6] The first Hong Kong SAR Chief Executive after handover in 1997 Mr. Tung Chee-Hwa (1997–2002), a shipping magnate, was quoted as having said in a 2002 interview that universal suffrage for Hong Kong could possibly be considered after 2012. This glimmer of hope for many Hong Kongers was dashed by the PRC government in 2012 when they announced plans for rotating leadership, but gave no firm timetable for implementing universal suffrage.

Kong government which feature a 16% flat personal rate for everyone, an 18% flat tax rate for corporations, and no capital gains tax. The people of Hong Kong also take pride in its world class airport which leads the world in international air cargo. Its renown port facilities rank fifth in the world in container traffic (just behind Shenzhen [3rd] and ahead of Guangzhou [7th]). Its modern and pristine subway system, the Hong Kong Mass Transit Rail (MTR), moves over 5 million passengers per day within the urban area and is the envy of most cities in Asia. Finally, the communications systems within Hong Kong with connectivity to almost any area of the world are key to its prowess as the leading financial city in Asia. Most sacredly Hong Kongers all gather around their tradition of "rule of law." In essence, Hong Kong has become over the years since the end of World War II the closest thing that resembles pure capitalism on this planet. It was a system left behind by a series of mostly competent British Colonial Governors appointed by the Crown dating back to 1842.

However, no system is perfect and no system in history has ever been immune from external or internal factors that can potentially lead to its eventual demise. In the case of Hong Kong there are obvious cracks on the wall that have appeared as we enter the 23rd year of "one country, two systems" dating back to retrocession to China in 1997. We are still 27 years shy of the expiration of the fifty year timetable which was announced in the 1984 Joint Sino-U.K. Declaration. A local business friend of mine who has managed a very successful export business the past two decades remarked to me recently, "During the period just prior to the signing of the 1984 agreement the Chinese leadership under Deng Xiao-Ping considered China to be so poor and living standards across China so far behind Hong Kong that it would take fifty years to catch up. Actually, mainland China and particularly the adjacent Guangdong Province (population: 113 million) have caught up and, in fact, in some areas of commerce, industry and social development they have surpassed Hong Kong in just twenty years."

Is Accelerating Hong Kong's Entry into the Greater Bay Area (GBA) a Possible Solution to Resolving the Current Crisis and, If Yes, Is It a Possible Solution to Hong Kong's Housing Crisis?

There is widespread feeling across all socio-economic strata in Hong Kong that the influence of the real estate tycoons in Hong Kong needs to be controlled and incentives launched to provide more housing at affordable prices. Land auctions in recent years have been too scarce. Despite the appearance of extremely high population density in Hong Kong's nearly 400 sq. mile territory and hilly topography which poses challenges to civil engineering and construction of residential buildings, there are vacant lands in Hong Kong's New Territories which could accommodate new housing. In Hong Kong only 24% of the land has been developed and, of this developed land, only 7% has been used for housing.[7] At present country parks and nature reserves account for 40% of Hong Kong's land. Singapore offers an interesting contrast where 14% of land is used for housing and 9% has been set aside for parks and nature reserves. Plainly said the Hong Kong government is greatly behind the eight ball in its effort to provide affordable housing to more of its citizens. It normally takes three to five years to construct residential estates. The current crisis needs immediate action.

It was not always this way. An interesting episode occurred in Hong Kong's history after the Hong Kong riots of 1966–1967. Historians will argue over the exact causes of the riots of the period but housing policy mistakes may have exacerbated the tensions which formed and erupted into violent clashes. Soon after the 1967 riots and the arrival of Hong Kong's 25th Governor, Murray MacLehose, a concerted effort by the colonial government was undertaken to support the disadvantaged and create a giant expansion of public housing. It was the centerpiece of MacLehoses's policy initiatives. MacLehose's government focused on areas such as more practical regulations concerning squatters who had fled to Hong Kong from China. The effectiveness of rent control policy

[7] Statistics provided by *South China Morning Post* in its April 4, 2017 article entitled "Hong Kong's housing situation is dire compared to Singapore's. Here's what must be done".

dating to 1947 and plot ratio policies that had been set in 1962 were re-examined. MacLehose's Ten Year Plan focused mainly on freeing up more land to accommodate more affordable housing and adopting a Home-ownership scheme (HOS) in 1978 intended to assist homeowners who gained affluence over time. MacLehose, known by the beloved nickname of "Jock the Sock," revolutionized social policies for the ordinary Hong Konger. He became the longest serving Hong Kong governor in Hong Kong's colonial history and possibly the most beloved. To this day he remains today in the eyes of many Hong Kong historians the "Father of Modern Hong Kong." Over 220,000 housing units were constructed under his tenure. By the time he departed Hong Kong in 1982, most of the hillside squatters set up by fleeing immigrants were gone and replaced by affordable public housing.

Other Hong Kong leaders since MacLehose, whether British governors under the waning years of the Crown or local Hong Kong leaders post-1997, have tried to capture the historical moment like MacLehose did. To date none have succeeded. The first Hong Kong SAR Chief Executive Tung Chee Hwa (1998–2003) tried mightily to expand public housing units after 1998. His goal was to build 85,000 new public housing units with the target of achieving 80% home ownership among the Hong Kong population. However, he was held in contempt by many of the real estate tycoons who sabotaged his plans and gleefully saw him exit the stage following the 2003 SARS crisis.[8] Under his successor, Chief Executive Donald Tsang (2005–2012), home supply plummeted dramatically and housing prices started to climb precipitously. Price escalation continued to soar under Tsang's replacement, Chief Executive Mr. C. Y. Leung (2012–2017). Current Hong Kong Chief Executive Carrie Lam made a pledge in October 2019 to construct 100,000 housing units by 2024 (Fig. 4.1).

Oxford educated Scotsman Murray MacLehose (1917–2000) became the 25th Hong Kong Governor in 1971 after serving earlier in his career in the U.K. intelligence corps and then later Ambassador to South Vietnam (1967–1971). In addition to his accomplishments in the housing sector, MacLehose recognized Chinese as one of the official languages of Hong

[8] An outbreak of Severe Acute Respiratory Syndrome (SARS) occurred in Hong Kong, mainland China, and parts of Southeast Asia during the first half of 2003 spawning fear of a pandemic. A total of 299 people died in Hong Kong that spring and up to nearly 1800 cases were diagnosed with SARS, spelling out a 17% fatality rate.

Fig. 4.1 Sir Murray MacLehose, the most beloved colonial Governor (1971–1982)

Kong, set up Hong Kong's Independent Commission Against Corruption (ICAC), started construction of the Mass Transit Rail (MTR), and established a network of country parks around Hong Kong's territory. In deference to the probable and eventual return of Hong Kong to Chinese sovereignty in 1997, he opposed significant changes under his tenure that would move Hong Kong towards constitutional democracy. Despite tense last minute Sino-British handover negotiations and the decision of high level British officials to boycott the handover ceremonies to China in July 1997, MacLehose and former British PM Edward Heath attended the official handover ceremonies in Hong Kong harbor.

A re-incarnation of Governor MacLehose aside, a bolder action that could be considered today, given the absence of the Cold War that existed in the later years of Hong Kong's colonial period, might even be to expand the Hong Kong S.A.R. boundary into Guangdong Province or conduct and encourage a quasi-open boarder policy through practical initiatives that would render access to affordable residential housing estates for Hong Kong residents. This solution, however, would require examination of how the "one country, two systems" legal structure applies. China has made stunning progress in its investment and development of rapid transit across China in recent years. Speed train rail lines recently opened in the past year now take only 15 minutes and 47 minutes respectively to Shenzhen and Guangzhou, the capital of Guangdong Province. The Hong Kong—Guangzhou train ride used to take nearly three hours. These new transportation links into mainland China have been intended to facilitate Hong Kong's integration into the Greater Bay Area.

How Can It Be Done in a Way That Lessens the Growing Gap Between Rich and Poor in Hong Kong?

A recent business forum in Hong Kong showed the staggering disproportion of wealth that has developed in recent years in Hong Kong. According to a recent report at the American Chamber of Commerce, companies controlled by the wealthiest 65 families in Hong Kong account for 75% of Hong Kong's Gross Domestic Product (GDP). Home ownership has been dropping for the past 15 years and now stands at only 48%.

How Can Reforms in Hong Kong Education Reduce the Divide That Is Emerging Within Hong Kong Society?

The reforms needed in education most critically should address "increasing chances for more" and staking out a "Hong Kong identity." Insisting that a greater portion of education be done in Mandarin could be helpful in preparing the large mass of students leaving the education system at age 18 either for more vocation work paths or later at age 22 for more professional skilled work. However, that is just part of the challenge. Currently only 18% of Hong Kong secondary school students are entering government funded university spots in Hong Kong.[9] Singapore, by comparison, admits approximately 26% of their secondary school graduates into government funded universities in Singapore. The Hong Kong figure of 18% is not only lower than Singapore, it is the lowest rate of admission among students in Macau, Hong Kong, Taiwan, and Singapore. Compared to OECD member countries as well, the Hong Kong

[9] Refer to May 2016 article "Hong Kong's growing shortage of university places" by journalist Matt Fleming regarding Hong Kong's shortage of university spaces.

figure is alarming. Comparative university admission rates in the U.S., Australia, Canada, and Sweden are approximately 68%.

Another area that has become quite sensitive in Hong Kong in recent years is the teaching of Chinese history. It appears there is emphasis on teaching Chinese history in Hong Kong schools mainly up until the fall of the Qing Dynasty in 1911 and the establishment of the Republic of China. All Chinese in Hong Kong, Taiwan, and mainland China agree that Dr. Sun Yat-Sen is the Father of modern China. Dr. Sun, who came from a Cantonese family and was also raised part of his childhood in Hawaii, is a unifying figure to all Chinese and viewed in their hearts and minds much in the same way that George Washington is revered in the United States. However, it appears there is not a consistent teaching approach to Chinese history following the legacy of Dr. Sun which would include the establishment of the Republic of China in the period following 1911. Chinese history from the fall of the Qing through the 1920s and 1930s with Japan's annexation of Manchuria and the outbreak of World War II in 1937 and the establishment of the Peoples Republic of China in 1949 is subject to many interpretations. The period under Mao's rule (1949–1976) is even at best glossed over in Chinese history books in mainland China today. It might be 100 years before the Chinese can accurately put Mao's controversial role in Chinese history into proper perspective. It is to this day difficult in mainland China to engage someone openly and publicly in a conversation about Mao. The excesses of the Great Leap Forward and ensuing famine, the Cultural Revolution (1966–1976), and economic take-off that started under Deng Xiao-Ping are also difficult to put into the same chapter of any history book.

However, the Hong Kong problem today, similar to one faced in Taiwan the past 40 years, is a challenge over how to recognize that one is both Chinese and yet retain one's local pride. In Taiwan when opposition DPP Party leader Chen Shui-Bian, a former Taiwan independence advocate and anti-government activist under Taiwan's martial law period 1949–1992, assumed the presidency in 2000, his administration sought to make Taiwanese dialect the medium of language instruction in Taiwan. He sought to assert the view that Taiwanese people were not Chinese. This view, taken to such an extreme, was one among many reasons that the presidency of Taiwan swung back in favor of the KMT Party under Harvard trained Ma Ying-Jeou in the 2008 election. Many in the Taiwan business community who had moved their factories to China in the 1990s when labor costs made Taiwan manufacturing in light industries uncompetitive, were at odds with Chen's radical policy. Subsequently the election of Ma in March 2008 with 58% of the vote showed that most Taiwanese, while remaining proud to retain vestiges of Taiwanese culture and lifestyle, could also consider themselves to be ethnically Chinese, too. Mandarin remains the language of learning in all the schools in Taiwan[10] except a few new pilot schools who are experimenting with the idea of bi-lingual education in both Mandarin and English. There is a tacit acknowledgement in Taiwan that the mainland Chinese economy will become the largest economy in the world within the coming decade and it would set back Taiwan university graduates if they were not fluent speakers of Mandarin.

Ma was succeeded in Taiwan by Ms. Tsai Ing-Wen a former National Taiwan University academic who also studied at London School of Economics. She is a DPP Party member and represents the pendulum swinging back toward a more "nativist" style of leadership in Taiwan. However, there is a joke in Taiwan that the 2nd largest Taiwanese city is Shanghai making humor of the fact that so many businessmen and women from Taiwan have moved to the bustling business center of Shanghai during the past 20 years. Many in the Taiwan business community take a pragmatic view (i.e. pragmatism over ideology!) that it would be unwise for Taiwan to assert its independence with so much investment into the mainland by Taiwan industrialists. What the movement of Taiwan and Hong Kong business operations into China reflects is the economic reality that Hong Kong, Taiwan, Macau, and China are de facto unified already. Economic unification has already occurred. Politics often lags a generation or so behind the economic realities. One can also carry on the debate over who have been the greater "agents of change"—the mainland Chinese or the overseas Chinese and Hong Kong businessmen who have come back to invest in the mainland? At one point in time in the late 1990s it was estimated that 70% of the foreign investment into China was either coming from overseas Chinese investing back into their ancestral home or Western corporations employing overseas Chinese to manage their China

[10] In a comparison of how Mandarin medium of learning in Taiwan, China and HK, and Singapore/Malaysia is viewed locally, in Taiwan Mandarin is called "guo yu" (or "the national language"). In China and HK, Mandarin is referred to as "putong hua" (or the "standard dialect"). In Singapore/Malaysia where the official national language is actually Malay, Mandarin is referred to as "hua yu" (the Chinese ethnic language).

based subsidiary. One cannot understate the tremendous impact the overseas Chinese (often referred to by mainland Chinese sympathetically as "hua qiao") have had on modernizing China's economy during the past 40 years.

Meanwhile back on the streets of Hong Kong protesters have spray painted the city in recent months with graffiti that often states "Take back Hong Kong!" and lambasted anything mainland Chinese in a condescending manner that suggests serious contempt for China. This is a tragedy. Hong Kong lies within one of the most vibrant economic zones in the world, yet its youth do not see themselves as part of it and are expressing frustrations of hopelessness. If Hong Kong students thought they had a bright future it is difficult to believe they would be out on the streets in such bitter and violent opposition to their government. Today in Hong Kong streets the protests are carried out largely in Cantonese dialect except for moments when CNN or BBC cameramen pass by and the protester chants quickly switch into English for dramatic effect. The protesters have attacked Hong Kong residents on the streets whom they believe may be from mainland China. Regrettably the atmosphere in Hong Kong in the second half of 2019 has become so toxic that many mainland Chinese and Taiwanese families living in Hong Kong have told their children or family members not to speak Mandarin in public when they are out on the streets. This base behavior by a radical minority within the protestors reflects a sad moment of xenophobia and intolerance in Hong Kong. It is a rarity for a city so long known for its embracement of cosmopolitan norms and general acceptance of cultural diversity. Mainland Chinese students and Taiwanese students and Korean students who were studying as foreign students were evacuated out the back door of Chinese University of Hong Kong onto boats on the waterfront side of the school campus in late November 2019 when campus rioting reached such a state of frenzy that they were prevented from safely exiting out the front gates of the university campus.

Reforms in education that would program the young people in Hong Kong for success after they graduate from secondary schools and university are essential. Beyond the needed skillset, the focus on a new Hong Kong identity that can be both proudly Cantonese and Chinese and global citizen is even more crucial. The impression at present, whether deserved or not, is that Hong Kong's education system has missed the mark with this generation of high school and university graduates. The educational system has not sufficiently evolved since handover in 1997 to address the opportunities and skill sets needed for Hong Kong youth in the new modern economy. Serious review and self-examination is needed. Are young Hong Kong graduates truly competitive with their counterparts in other areas around Asia from Taiwan, Singapore, and Malaysia? One must seek truth from the facts in order to properly analyze the current situation.

Hong Kong and Shenzhen in 1980

The Pearl River Delta looked quite differently in 1980 compared to today. Hong Kong was the booming gateway to China; Shenzhen was hardly a household name anyone would remember. In fact, the city was officially established only in 1979 taking its name from a former mainland county town in Bao An County located on the Hong Kong Colonial boundary. On the old Canton (Guangzhou) to Hong Kong train line (a train ride I suffered through with my wife lasting 6 hours in 1983), the train station in today's Shenzhen was the last stop before pulling into Hong Kong. The impetus for Shenzhen's enormous leap into the Twenty-First Century began with the establishment of five Special Economic Zones (SEZs)[11] by the post-Maoist Beijing government under the leadership of Deng Xiao-Ping in 1980. Shenzhen was the first SEZ to be set up and the Beijing authorities blessed its establishment by making it a tax-free zone. Foreign investors were encouraged to set up manufacturing and business operations in the newly minted city. At the time Shenzhen boasted a population of hardly 30,000 residents compared to Hong Kong's 6 million residents at the time.

However, within a period of 5 years there were over 500 factories setting up operations within the 675 square mile designated area of Shenzhen SEZ. Infrastructure set up rapidly to match the pace of industrial investment into Shenzhen. One measure of development at the time would be to trace the development of the Hong Kong—Guangzhou Expressway built by Princeton educated Hong Kong architect/entrepreneur, Gordon Wu. Wu, son of a Wanchai taxi driver and self-made man, laid forth the vision of building at a cost of over USD

[11] The first five Special Economic Zones (SEZs) set up by the PRC government after 1980 were Shenzhen, Shantou, and Zhuhai in Guangdong Province and Xiamen in Fujian Province. Hainan Island was also broken off from Guangdong Province to become a both a new province and special economic zone.

100 million an expressway that extends today over 60 miles between Hong Kong and the provincial capital, Guangzhou, passing along the way through the heart of Shenzhen and another key GBA city, Dongguan. As the crow flies, the expressway's geographical starting point was just 8 miles from downtown Hong Kong just across the mainland China-Hong Kong border. The expressway construction was started in 1987 and opened for business in 1997. The first year of its operation, the expressway under its new name, Guangshen Expressway, averaged about 16,000 cars per day. That figure quickly expanded to 32,000 cars by its third year of operation and today averages over 60,000 cars per day.

The number of factories built in Shenzhen's Special Economic Zone (SEZ) grew to over 20,000 by the year 2000 and its population by then had grown to just over 4 million. With a tidal wave of economic growth now unleashed the city of Shenzhen reached a population of 8 million by the end of 2010. Actually since 2010, Shenzhen has started to see a decline in factory operations as the price of real estate in the city has soared and worker's wages in Shenzhen now also make it like a modern day version of "a 1980s Hong Kong." Essentially, it has become less competitive to manufacture in Shenzhen than in some of the more remote areas of Guangdong Province. In the most recent decade labor costs in some of the nascent cities in the province began taking over the manufacturing role. Cities like Dongguan, Jiangmen, Foshan, Zhongshan, and Zhuhai have taken over Shenzhen's manufacturing as transportation and communication links have made it possible for more companies to venture further inland into the mainland in search of cheaper labor costs. Once a manufacturing hub during the Deng Xiao Ping era, today Shenzhen has morphed into one of China most sophisticated hi-tech research and development hubs.

The 1980s and 1990s saw a steady flow of Chinese migrating from inner, poorer provinces in mainland China to Shenzhen in order to lay claim to their piece of opportunity. Today the population of Shenzhen has soared to 12.5 million residents, making it 60% more populous than Hong Kong. Its subway system has a vast network of metro lines covering most of the urban area. Shenzhen's boundaries are sprawling and extend over 800 square miles making its land size approximately double that of Hong Kong. The transit system links seamlessly into its sparkling new airport that services most major provincial cities in mainland China. By 2017, the GDP of Shenzhen reached USD 338 billion, surpassing the

Table 4.1 Major Economic indicators of the Greater Bay Area (2017)

City	*Land Area (sq km)*	*Population (inn)*	*GDP (USD bn)*	*Per-capita GDP (USD)*	*Tertiary industry share of GDP (%)*	*Exports (USD bn)*	*Utilized FDI (USD bn)*[b]
GBA	**55,906**	**69.6**	**1513.4**	**21,750**	**65.6**	**1090.2**	**140.7**
Hong Kong[a]	1106	7.4	341.4	46,190	*92.2*	497.3	117.4
Macao[a]	31	0.7	50.4	77,600	*93.4*	1.4	1.5
Guangzhou	7249	14.5	318.2	22,320	70.9	85.7	6.3
Shenzhen	1997	12.5	332.0	27,120	58.6	244.6	7.4
Foshan	3798	7.7	141.3	18,450	40.1	46.7	1.6
Dongguan	2460	8.3	112.2	13,530	52.3	104.0	1.7
Huizhou	11,347	4.8	56.7	11,880	40.7	33.0	1.1
Zhongshan	1784	3.3	51.1	15,750	47.8	30.4	0.5
Jiangmen	9505	4.6	39.8	8740	44.7	15.9	0.5
Zhuhai	1736	1.8	38.0	22,100	48.0	27.9	2.4
Zhaoqing	14,891	4.1	32.6	7940	38.3	3.3	0.2

Notes [a]DP shares of tertiary industry for Hong Kong and Macao are 2016 figures; [b]2017 average exchange rates for USD 1 are HKD 7.794, RMB 6.759, MOP 8.026; Hong Kong exports include re-exports of goods sourced from or destined for the Chinese Mainland, mostly the PRD Area
Source Creating the Greater Bay Area of the Future-Opportunities for Hong Kong by Dr. Michael J. Enright and the 2022 foundation/HK Trade Dev. Council, Statistics of the Guangdong-Hong Kong Macao Bay Area (2018)

GDP of both Hong Kong and Singapore.[12] That is the story of the rise of a fishing village of less than 30,000 residents to 12.5 million within a 40 year time period. There has literally been nothing like it in modern history (Table 4.1).

[12]According to *South China Morning Post*, Shenzhen's 2017 annual GDP figure at USD 320 billion surpassed Hong Kong's USD 330 billion and Singapore's USD 305 billion.

CHAPTER 5

Law and Order: The Future of Rule of Law in the Greater Bay Area

Abstract This chapter traces the historical difficulty with which both the Chinese and British government authorities have ruled over Guangdong Province and Hong Kong. It also highlights the legal implications of the English "common law" legacy in Hong Kong versus the "civil law" legal tradition from Europe that took root earlier in China. The chapter analyses the critical importance of language policy and educational policies and their potential to glue or un-glue a society using Switzerland and the former Yugoslavia as examples.

Keywords Hong Kong under Qing Dynasty · The Opium Wars · Hong Kong's colonial period · Hong Kong SAR under Basic Law

As one contemplates the role of rule of law in Hong Kong and the Greater Bay Area in the foreseeable future it might be useful to review some moments of past history. Let us analyze how both the Chinese leadership

B. VonCannon, *Status Anxiety*,
https://doi.org/10.1007/978-981-15-7028-5_5

in Beijing and the British government in London viewed Hong Kong and how to manage it.

The Past: Hong Kong and Guangdong Province During the Chinese Dynastic Period (Pre-1911)

One can only embark upon an analysis of Chinese dynastic history in small portions at a time. Since its inception over 2000 years ago, China has endured more than 550 emperors through the span of over a dozen major dynasties that ended in 1911 with the overthrow of the Qing Dynasty and the establishment of the Republic of China. If you are chatting with well-read Chinese friends at a dinner party, you might ask them their opinion of the greatest dynasties in Chinese history. It is my guess they might say the Tang Dynasty (609-907 A.D.) was the greatest as it was a period when China's borders stretched significantly across Asia and it was also a golden age in art and culture. Historical accounts of the Tang suggest an indifference to southern neighbors in the Guangdong Region when the city of Guangzhou was sacked and burned by Persian and Arab traders in 758 A.D. An even more brutal event occurred under the Tang reign in 878-79 A.D. termed the "Guangzhou Massacre" when the rebel army of warlord General Huang Chao attempted to overthrow the Tang Dynasty and was violently suppressed with estimates of loss of life at 100,000 or more.

Hong Kong at that time was not yet on any map and would not surface in historical accounts until the late 1700s. The key trading estuary of the region was the Pearl River and the focal point where ships docked were in the upper reaches of the river at Canton (today's Guangzhou)! By the year 1500, Portuguese traders had begun establishing a trading post in Macao further to the south which had deeper waters than the Pearl River near Guangzhou and was more convenient to the larger hulk European ships. Macao was a small island just off the tip of the mainland in the area where the mainland city of Zhuhai is located today.

Hong Kong biographer, Frank Welsh, further chronicles attitudes toward Guangdong province under the successors of the Tang, the Sung Dynasty, who characterized it as being "an odd region, regarded by the rest of China with suspicion and disdain. The Sung emperors, who ruled from 960 to 1279, were worried by reports of the great number of wizards and sorcerers in the city (of Guangzhou)." Welsh notes accounts from a Sung imperial diary alluding to "its remoteness, (one thousand two hundred miles) from Peking (Beijing) and separated by numerous mountain ranges as well as the language spoken by the inhabitants is unintelligible to northern Chinese. Furthermore, their customs are looked upon with distaste. It seems Cantonese will eat anything—including bats, tortoises, raw monkey-brains, and new-born rats."

Hong Kong During the Qing Dynasty (1644–1911)

The Qing Dynasty, established in 1644, ranks as probably the third most influential dynasty after the Han (220 BC to 220 AD) and the Tang (609 AD to 907 AD). Early years of the Qing Dynasty were notable for their accomplishments. The 2nd Qing Emperor, Kangxi, who would rule for 61 years until 1722 is considered perhaps the greatest of all Chinese emperors. His grandson, Qian Long, the 4th Qing emperor also ranks highly for his leadership and ruled over a prosperous era that touched the origins of Hong Kong in the late 1790s. Modern history has been largely unkind to the later years of the Qing Dynasty owing to its monumental fall from grace during the last hundred years of rule and the periods of humiliation that its leaders allowed to be brought upon China. China's image in the eyes of the world dropped precipitously following the sequence of events under Qing rule namely the two Opium Wars (1839–1842 and 1856–1860), the Taiping Rebellion (1850–1864), The Boxer Rebellion (1899–1901), and a humiliating defeat suffered at the hands of the invading Japanese army. Most notably in the Sino-Japanese War of 1894–1895 the Empress Dowager squandered China's military budget in order to re-build the Summer Palace in Beijing depriving the Chinese military of munitions at a critical time during the conflict. Much of this decadence of power is reflected in Italian film maker Bernardo Bertolucci's 1987 hit "The Last Emperor" which depicted the life of Pu Yi (the Xuan Tong Emperor) who was the last Qing Emperor and overthrown at the age of six during the aftermath of the 1911 Revolution. However, the greatness of the Qing should not be discounted. China's borders expanded significantly during their 267 years of rule and their deftness of diplomacy particularly in the early years of Qing rule should not be disparaged by historians.

One aspect of the Qing Dynasty which is relevant to our discussion about Hong Kong centers around the fact that the Qing were, in fact, not even Han Chinese.[1] They descended from the Manchu race (or also called Tartars) and were from the northern China area formerly referred to as Manchuria which today comprises China's three most northeastern provinces.[2] The Manchus conquered China from the north overthrowing the Ming Dynasty in 1644 who were essentially Han Chinese. The Manchus, a warring northern ethnicity inferior in numbers to the Ming, gained control over a vast mainland Chinese empire that had been weakened by widespread famine. At that time China had a population approaching 300 million, almost equal to the entire US population today. The Manchus, despite conquering the Han Chinese would over time (and greatly abetted by intermarriage and adoption of Chinese customs) become assimilated into Han Chinese culture rather than vice versa. A second quality worth noting is that Manchus were cautious and at times distrustful of the outside world, particularly the Jesuit missionaries who were seeking to spread their faith throughout Asia. The Manchus moved populations back from coastal areas, largely to protect their borders but also in concert with policies that sought to minimize contact with the outside world. As a result of these policies, Guangzhou was designated as the only city under the Qing Dynasty that was officially permitted to conduct trade with the outside world. This highlighted the importance of Guangzhou. To this day in the eyes of most Chinese, Shanghai has historically been considered the leading business center within China owing to its central location and proximity to the Yangtse River that flows through the heartland of China. However, Guangzhou's role in establishing trade with the Western world has always been considered the earliest and most formidable.

The earliest maritime trade routes into China from the West were set up by the Portuguese in the 1500s. In such light, Macao, was the earliest foreign enclave associated with China trade, not Hong Kong. Portugal's fortunes early on became significant in the new world in Asia but plummeted significantly during the 1700s when it was blocked out of Japan by the policies of the Tokugawa Period. As this was occurring, Great

[1] China consists of five major historically important ethnic groups and several sub-ethnic peoples. The five majors would be the Han, the Manchus, the Mongols, the Uyghurs, and the Tibetans. Approximately 92% of Chinese are descendent from Han culture. Despite dynastic rule by the Mongols (Yuan dynasty) and Manchus (Qing Dynasty) over time Han culture has absorbed these influences.

[2] The three Manchurian provinces are Jilin, Liaoning, and Heilongjiang.

Britain became the most prominent nation on the rise (despite the loss of its North American colonies in 1780s). By the late 1700s Britain had worked itself into a position of significance controlling most of the trade into the port of Canton (today called Guangzhou) which remained the sole Chinese port officially sanctioned by the Qing Dynasty royal court to be open for foreign trade.

With the flow of trade between China and the outside world confined to the city of Guangzhou, trade between China and Great Britain began to grow precipitously in the mid-1700s under the 4th Qing Emperor, Qian Long, who ruled for sixty years until self-abdicating in 1796.[3] Chronicled records of the time laud the orderly manner with which the Manchus organized trade with the outside world. They slowly became to realize its value but sought to keep out the cultural influence of foreigners whom they deemed inferior to themselves. The trading season at the time was restricted to six months of the year. Foreigners were permitted to live in Guangzhou but only in a restricted area of the city where warehouses were allowed to be constructed. Sound familiar? This would set a precedent which would be practiced a century and half later at the Canton Trade Fairs which were set up in 1957 in Guangzhou when Mao Tse-Tung re-initiated trade with the outside world under the Peoples Republic of China (PRC) government after having shut the door on outside world for nearly a decade following the 1949 revolution. The Canton Trade Fairs, too, were held for a short season (in the spring) just like in the late 1700s. It should be noted as well that the foreign community allowed into China during the Canton trade season in the early Nineteenth Century were restricted to an all-male policy only. Western women were strictly not allowed. In fact, years later in the 1830s when Sino-British trade tensions were regrettably to reach a flash point, an incident occurred in 1834 when a prominent British trader brought his wife ashore and this incident greatly increased tensions with the Qing Dynasty officials in Guangzhou.

A regrettable side to the history of this time was the rise of opium trade. The British sought desperately to bring to market products which would allow them to import more Chinese goods such as silk, spices,

[3] Qian Long abdicated in 1796 out of deep respect for his grandfather, Kangxi, who ruled for 61 years (1644–1722) as he did not wish to eclipse the length of rule nor the greatness of his grandfather. Qian Long remained the de facto ruler of China until his death in 1799 but officially ceded power in 1796.

and ceramics and stem the flow of silver out of the British Empire. By the late 1700s through the East India Company the British began to bring to market opium which at the time was not considered an outlawed substance in Great Britain. This product seemed to have particular appeal in China. Records by the early traders at the time show brisk demand for opium which expanded from 4000 chests per year in 1790 to 20,000 chests by 1810 and 44,000 chests by 1830. In fact, by 1830 Manchu authorities in both Guangzhou and Peking had become alarmed with the spread of opium use throughout China and the alarming rate of addiction among the population. Emperor Jia Qing, 5th Emperor and successor to Qian Long, who ruled between 1796 and 1820, began to seek restrictions on trade with the U.K. government as a means of stopping the pervasive spread of opium usage throughout China.

Regrettably as the opium trade continued to grow, the amount of corruption of government officials throughout China became more pervasive as well. It was during these pivotal years in the early 1800s that Hong Kong first gained a presence on maritime maps. As the authorities in Guangzhou sought to ban the trade of opium, British ships sought out little enclaves along the Pearl River entry where they would lay anchor waiting for the precipitous moment for unloading their contraband. One of their favoring moorings was at the Kowloon wharf area which is just meters away from today's Star Ferry pier on the Kowloon Peninsula where large leisure cruise boats often dock.

Regrettably under Emperor Jia Qing's successor, Dao Guang, trade ties with Great Britain continued to worsen and he sought to sever trading ties completely with Great Britain in the late 1830s. It resulted in hostilities breaking out in 1839 between the British who insisted on the right to conduct trade and the Chinese who wished to stop the opium trade. The result of these hostilities was the First Opium War (1839–1842) which was dominated by Great Britain's superior naval might and resulted in the signing of the Treaty of Nanking (1842) by the humiliated Qing Dynasty government. Under the terms of the treaty China was to cede control of the island of Hong Kong to Great Britain in perpetuity and to lease the Kowloon peninsula for a period of 150 years.

How Did the British Maintain Law and Order Under the British Colonial Period from 1842 to 1997?

Following the conclusion of the First Opium War in 1842 and the humiliating defeat of the Qing Dynasty by the British, the UK government consolidated its grip over Hong Kong by setting up a colonial government that was led by a Governor who was appointed by the British Crown. Its first governor, former Lt. General Henry Pottinger was installed in 1843. He was to be succeeded by a series of 27 Governors culminating with the last colonial governor, Chris Patten, who served as Hong Kong Governor from 1993 until the territory was handed over to China in 1997. The Hong Kong Colonial Governor served at the pleasure of the British government in London. He was aided by a colonial administration of civil servants who managed the development of Hong Kong ensuring its safety through a colonial police force and army troops stationed in garrison locally. The colonial governor's powers encompassed the authority to build of public roads, port facilities, and the establishment of health standards and exercising fiduciary responsibility over a treasury that levied taxes and met government budgets.

Under the British Crown, local residents in Hong Kong enjoyed many of the same rights as the citizens of the United Kingdom. These rights included the first tier of constitutional rights that included free speech, the right of assembly, freedom of religion, and encouraging an open and free market economy. In fact, as British Overseas subjects they enjoyed the right to immigrate anywhere within the British commonwealth until laws changed this status in 1981.

There seems to be a blurring and exaggeration about the colonial period that ended in 1997 as we have moved further away from it. First of all, antagonists of the current Hong Kong government make claims that it has snuffed out democracy and is threatening the rule of law. One might beg to differ with this assessment, however, if we examine the degree to which the United Kingdom actually established democracy in Hong Kong. Aside from the first-tier democratic rights listed above, for the bulk of the 150 years of British Colonial Rule there was no universally elected parliamentary body.

The issue of universal suffrage and greater enfranchisement of the local (largely) Chinese population remained retarded for most of the British Colonial period. Periods of tension over these two issues are recorded throughout Hong Kong's colonial history. The Social Ordinance of 1884 targeted local chambers of commerce and banned free association of workers in unions perhaps as a reaction to the series of coolie strikes that had occurred in Hong Kong in the years 1844, 1858, 1862–1863, and 1872. As early as 1896 requests were made by a group of local residents and merchants seeking to allow a plebiscite and constitutional changes permitting majority rule on Hong Kong's Sanitary Board which oversaw aspects of the territory's sanitary and health practices. However, it was rejected by the Hong Kong Governor at the time, Sir William Robinson. Eventually in 1936 the Sanitary Board would be re-named the Urban Council, a political body that was phased out in 1999 following retrocession with powers and duties ceded to the District Councils.

A more notable event in Hong Kong's evolution toward more democratic rule occurred in 1946 under Hong Kong Governor Mark Young. Young's bold plan proposed setting up a 48-member Municipal Council that would be composed one-third non-chinese, one-third Chinese institutional representatives, and one-third individuals. Governor Young wished to accord greater freedom and inclusiveness in the governing of Hong Kong. However, he was to find opposition within his local administration and, particularly, within the military ranks who engineered his ouster as Governor in 1947. Young was replaced by career colonial officer Alexander Grantham who promptly blocked Young's reform agenda. With the Great Britain having fallen into the throes of a post-World War II recession up until 1952 and Winston Churchill having returned to power under Tory leadership, Governor Grantham allowed plans for widespread political reform in Hong Kong to go un-approved in London in an atmosphere that had become increasingly influenced by the Cold War and the post-1949 Chinese Communist leadership in Beijing under the leadership of Mao Tse-Tung (Figs. 5.1 and 5.2).

The Urban Council did undergo some limited reform in 1952. This body was empowered to oversee cleaning, bath house supervision, public toilets, and cemeteries. The government acceded to expanding the number of elected seats on the Urban Council from two to four. At the time the Hong Kong population was expanding rapidly to approximately 1 million. It would be a far cry to say that universal suffrage existed in Hong Kong. The numbers of residents who qualified to vote was approximately 9000. It would later expand to 250,000 by 1966 and 500,000 by 1981.

Fig. 5.1 Sir Mark Aitchison Young, 21st colonial Governor of Hong Kong. There were differing views about the future rule of Hong Kong within the Hong Kong Colonial Government. Cambridge educated Sir Mark Aitchison Young (Fig. 5.1) served as Hong Kong Governor before the war and returned to office after the Japanese Occupation of Hong Kong. He presented the Young Plan in 1946 laying forth greater inclusiveness by the local residents only to have it scaled back under the leadership of Alexander Grantham (Fig. 5.2), a Sandhurst graduate and career colonial administrator, who became Hong Kong Governor in 1947

In summary, political swings within the colonial government to more populous styles only to be followed by swings back to more hardline, authoritarian colonial rule in post-World War II Hong Kong has been the rule more than the exception. Hong Kong's role in U.K. foreign policy dating to the late Nineteenth Century often occupied a controversial place. Some in the British foreign office even advocated early return of Hong Kong to Chinese sovereignty so as to avoid having it stand in the way of maintaining a harmonious trade relationship with China.

Fig. 5.2 Sir Alexander Grantham, 22nd colonial Governor of Hong Kong

Some have even taken the view that Hong Kong was really a "Chinese colony" administered by the British as it did not fit the normal demographic of a traditional colony like, let's say, North America or Australia which were initially colonies founded by a European race that migrated in large numbers to a new land. Hong Kong has always been predominantly home to Chinese residents. In light of the most recent street protests in Hong Kong occurring in 2014 with the Occupy Hong Kong movement and followed in 2019 by unparalleled street violence, vandalism, and destruction, it might be useful to examine a similar period of unrest that occurred in 1966–1967. In mid-1966 Hong Kong became rocked by serious street rioting and bombings instigated by local communist cells who were inspired by the Cultural Revolution on the mainland. The catalysts for these riots were set off by an increase in the price of tickets for the Star Ferry boats which cross Victoria harbor throughout each day. This was a day and age before the first harbor crossing tunnel was built and the Star Ferry was a critical transportation link in Hong Kong.[4] The ticket fare increase impacted many of the workers who commuted back and forth each day from the Kowloon Peninsula to Hong Kong island. Outbreaks in violence resulted in Hong Kong Governor David Trench calling out the British Armed forces from their military barracks in Hong Kong to quell the violence. In the ensuing 18 months of unrest over 50 Hong Kong residents died in the street struggles that erupted, many deaths resulting from a series of bombings that occurred.

How Have the Chinese Maintained Law and Order Since 1997?

Chinese sovereignty over Hong Kong since the 1997 retrocession has been guided by the Basic Law document drafted jointly by Chinese and British negotiators and released at the signing of the 1984 Joint Sino-British Declaration. It essentially prescribes a "one country, two systems" approach which will last for fifty years (until 2047). Rival political parties are allowed to exist in Hong Kong, the two largest being the DAB (Democratic Alliance for the Betterment and Progress of Hong Kong), a pro-Beijing Party set up in 1992 and the Pan-Democratic Party and other smaller parties which have been aligned with the pro-democracy movement in recent years.

Whether or not the Hong Kong SAR government has been abiding by the doctrine of the Basic Law has been a topic of intense debate between the political parties in Hong Kong and subject to intense local and international press scrutiny. Before passing judgement on whether or not the Hong Kong government is toeing the line properly, it might be useful to examine Hong Kong's economic development since 1997.

It is undeniable that the Beijing government has contributed vast resources toward improving the infrastructure of Hong Kong. Hong Kong's Mass Transit Railway (or commonly called "MTR" locally), which was opened under the British Colonial period in 1979 with one subway line, today consists of multiple lines and over 160 MTR stations covering

[4] The earliest of Hong Kong's three cross- harbour tunnels was opened to traffic in 1972 connecting Hung Hom on Kowloon side of the harbour to Causeway Bay on the Hong Kong island side. Over 100,000 vehicles pass through it daily. An Eastern Harbor crossing tunnel was opened in 1989 and a Western Harbour Crossing tunnel was opened in 1997.

a length of 135 miles and moving just under 5 million Hong Kong residents daily. The trains today have air-conditioning as do most of Hong Kong's public buses and taxis and harbor ferries. Hong Kong remains perhaps the easiest city in Asia for moving from one location to another within the urban area and surrounding territories. It is a model of efficiency. In addition, train and auto links into China were dramatically improved in 2018 by the completion of the USD 11 billion speed train project connecting Hong Kong to Guangzhou and Fujian Province as well as the USD 18.8 billion Hong Kong-Zhuhai-Macao bridge. These projects have created two new arteries for rapid transport to and from mainland China in addition to the existing train lines and roads that existed prior to 1997.

Sanitation standards in Hong Kong today are far better than they were under the Britain Colonial period. The 2003 SARS crisis which plunged the city into a full-blown economic crisis eventually resulted in a mandate to clean up the city and significantly raise health standards. As this book went to print, the outbreak of a severe virus in early 2020 known as the Coronavirus (Covid-19) in the centrally located mainland China city of Wuhan (approximately 2 hours by direct flight from Hong Kong) gave cause for global health authorities to issue a global health emergency alert. Hong Kong authorities were very quick to react and seek to restrict air, sea, and land travel in and out of mainland China as well as quarantine persons believed to have been exposed to the virus. Isolated cases of persons contracting the virus had occurred and were being treated locally in Hong Kong. Hong Kong authorities had learned a great deal about mobilizing for pandemics under the SARS crisis in 2003 and it seemed at the outset of the threat wrought by Covid-19 to be at the forefront of countries and territories adept at adopting appropriate measures for its containment. As the epicenter of the coronavirus has moved to Europe and North America, the statistics available to date show the government of Hong Kong, the medical community, emergency rescue personnel, the police department, and ordinary citizens have banded together to combat the deadly in an effective manner. In early spring, as infection rates in New York City rose above 160,000 residents and death toll exceeded 10,000, Hong Kong with a population roughly the same as New York and a population density much higher than New York had held infections to approximately 1000 residents and a death toll under 10. It is remarkable how the city has put aside political differences for this greater cause and shown resiliency and civic discipline to meet this life or death challenge.

Environmental critics in Hong Kong will argue with some justification that the air quality locally is often more deficient today than in years past. Certain days of the year when the sea winds blow from the north, Hong Kong is likely to become covered with smog drifting over from the thousands of factories in areas of Guangdong Province. The Hong Kong Weather Observatory's capable monitoring of air quality each day allows schools to keep children indoors on days when air quality index level is at unhealthy levels. The observatory reliably tracks typhoon storms in the May to October period each year and has an excellent warning system procedure that has saved many lives in the past from destructive winds and flooding.

Some Western journalists notably have argued that China's rise during the past 40 years has come at the expense of Hong Kong. From an economic growth point of view nothing could be further from the truth. Hong Kong's GDP has grown robustly from USD 29 billion in 1980 to USD 363 billion in 2018, an average annual expansion of 6.9%. Starting from the 1997 retrocession year when Hong Kong's GDP was USD 177 billion, it has more than doubled over that 22 year period. The Hong Kong Stock Exchange has also enjoyed stellar growth as well. It had a market capitalization of USD 413 billion in 1997 and today HKEX's capitalization has reached USD 3.9 trillion, a 900% increase in 22 years. Pundits can justifiably argue over the fairness of the distribution of wealth in Hong Kong today and how it can and must be improved. However, it is hard to deny the reality of enormous economic progress that has occurred in Hong Kong since 1997. It is equally hard to deny mainland China's impressive economic growth has not been a positive ingredient for Hong Kong's economic achievements.

Extending into the Greater Bay Area

When one hears "one country, two systems" one is apt to think of Basic Law and the blueprint laid forth in the 1984 Sino-British Agreement. However, if one thinks more abstractly about "one country, two systems" China has already been applying such practical approach within mainland China and parts of its domestic economy for the past 40 years. Consider the devastating impact of Maoist policies on the Chinese economy at the end of the Cultural Revolution. Post-Mao under the Deng Xiao-Ping era in the late 1970s and early 1980s, China began to apply a "one economy, two systems" approach initially in the agricultural sector of its economy. The agricultural reforms were so stunningly effective that the Beijing government increasingly looked at the market as a guiding force for implementing policy changes. Later the same approach was applied with the set-up of special economic zones (SEZs) along China's coastline. "One economy, two systems" within mainland China led to staggering GDP growth in areas of the country where the SEZs were set up. Then later reform of the state owned enterprises (SOEs) under Premier Zhu Rong-Ji's tenure (1998–2003) resulted in China downsizing the state owned sector by 40 million jobs.[5] It was Deng's successor, President Jiang Ze-Min, and Premier Zhu's goal to secure more growth in the mainland economy via the proliferation of the private sector. One could point to the Asian miracle economies of the 1970s, especially the "four tiger economies" (Singapore, Hong Kong, Taiwan, and South Korea) as having great influence on the economic decision making in Beijing in the early post-Maoist years. It is no secret that Deng Xiao-Ping particularly liked the reforms of Singapore Prime Minister Lee Kuan-Yew[6] and consulted with him frequently throughout the 1980s and 1990s.

It begs the question should the concept of "one country, two systems" be narrowly defined within a political context only or taken to be a general approach which has elements of political reform, economic reform, educational reform, and social reform. Clearly there are differences between Beijing's definition of "one country, two systems" and the definition espoused by many of the protesters in the streets of Hong Kong. The protestors largely rally around the flag of universal suffrage. China has not acquiesced to that degree of political autonomy. However, in terms of economic policy, China has been practicing a "one economy, two systems" approach since the 1980s and Hong Kong's economy has expanded rapidly during that time period.

[5] Harvard Scholar William Overholt compares Prime Minister Zhu's downsizing the SOEs by 40 million jobs to be the equivalent to eliminating 3 million jobs in the United States.

[6] Cambridge educated Lee Kuan-Yew led Singapore to nationhood in 1965 following Singapore's withdrawl from the Malaysian Federation. He is recognized among overseas Chinese as well as mainland Chinese as one of the great statesmen of the late Twentieth Century and early years of the new millennium.

The independent judiciary is a hallmark of Hong Kong's legal system. In my days as a banker we used to lament the differences in financial documentation between our offices in Hong Kong and Singapore where English "common law" tradition prevailed versus contracts in Taiwan, Korea, China, and Switzerland where the legal systems evolved out of the European Napoleonic or "civil law" legal tradition. We had to be on our toes as banking officers to ensure clients signed the appropriate documents relevant to the domicile and legal code where the transaction occurred. Today these differences in legal system may possibly be a reason why the "one country, two systems" debate has been viewed so differently by government authorities and by critics and protestors on the streets of Hong Kong. Noted Hong Kong University Professor Richard Wong, has made the observation that legal systems reflect different styles of control over economic and social activities.[7] The common law system (like what is practiced in Hong Kong) seeks to support private and market-originated initiatives. Civil Law (like what is practiced in mainland China) seeks state-desired outcomes. Civil law, Wong asserts, originated in France and is "policy implementing" and it is more often applied by "top down approach." It embraces socially-conditioned private contracting. Common law, by contrast, originated in England and is "dispute resolving" and supports unconditioned contracting. It also is more synonymous with implementing via a "bottom up approach." Wong observes that Macao has probably adapted more easily than Hong Kong to its retrocession back to China because Macao's territory was introduced to civil law in the Sixteenth Century by its early Portuguese colonists and that very civil law tradition is closer to what exists on the mainland. The argument for Hong Kong continuing its common law tradition is that it seems historically to be better suited for financial markets allowing them more legal independence essential to ensure that they thrive and flourish. London, located under a common law jurisdiction, is an international financial center, but Paris and Frankfurt (civil law domiciles) are not. In Asia, the two most thriving international financial centers are Hong Kong and Singapore which both operate under a common law tradition, not Taipei and Seoul who are largely influenced by civil law tradition.

According respect for a civil law system as it has continued to develop and evolve in mainland China seems justifiable, too. A common fallacy

[7] See "Different legal traditions keep Hong Kong and China apart" appearing in the "The View" by Professor Richard Wong, October 6, 2015.

by Western media is to continue to hold on to a Manichean approach toward China when it comes to reform. Clearly China has prioritized economic reform over other political and social reforms the past forty years. However, this is largely the same economic model successfully used by other Asian economies including Taiwan, South Korea, and Singapore. During the Cold War period we often viewed South Korea, Taiwan, and Singapore as holding on to the ideals of western democracy and free market. A more factual historical assessment is that economic reform preceded political and social reform in these three economies. These three economies have faced similar challenges as to what pace to open reforms in the political and social spheres. During roughly the same time period examples of countries in Asia where political reform was always prioritized over economic reform, notably India, Philippines, and Thailand, do not serve as stellar examples of a development model that any country would envy to follow, much less China. They remain largely countries where economic elites and special interest groups have squashed economic reform that might have actually allowed a significant middle class to emerge. One might also bring up the example of Russia which had a similar chance to prioritize its reform agenda following the collapse of the former Soviet Union in 1992. Tragically Russia after breaking away from its republics under the old USSR chose to prioritize political reform over all other forms of reform. The chaos that followed under the Yeltsin administration for Russia were wealth depleting and highly disruptive. Russia's annual GDP dropped by 40% in the ensuing years in the 1990s immediately after the formation of the Commonwealth of Independent States (CIS) plunging almost all Russians into deep economic hardship.

Differences remain over what "one country, two systems" means when it comes to educational reform in Hong Kong as well. China has not rigidly enforced Mandarin education in Hong Kong. However, one must ask if today that has been to the advantage or disadvantage of Hong Kong youth. If one speaks with a cross section of executive recruiters or human resources professionals they will lament the challenge they face seeking out competent Mandarin speakers among Hong Kong's youth. They will also underline the fact that English language standards in Hong Kong have deteriorated (not strengthened) among Hong Kong youth since 1997.[8] Some might, in fact, posit that China's benign negligence in the area of language education in Hong Kong has actually hurt Hong Kong youth. It might be useful to consider how Taiwan and Singapore handled this very issue in recent history. When Taiwan was returned to Chinese sovereignty in 1945 after 50 years of Japanese occupation, Mandarin was not widely spoken in Taiwan. Under the Japanese, Taiwanese had been allowed to speak their native dialect, Taiwanese (Hokkien), but all learning in schools was conducted in Japanese. After the KMT government retreated to Taiwan in 1949, the Republic of China-Taiwan government policies under Chiang Kai-Shek ruled with the widespread powers of "martial law" for forty years until 1988 and the educational policies called for implementing Mandarin language in schools. While Taiwanese dialect was accommodated, it was not encouraged. It was allowed only a limited number of hours on radio and television weekly. In fact, Taiwan has a small Hakka Chinese community in the Miaoli township area of the island. They, too, were to be allowed some allocation of air time for Hakka dialect on Taiwan radio and television periodically. However, it was very clear post-1949 in Taiwan that Mandarin would be the official language of Taiwan.

The Singapore language policy covered in Chapter 1 of this book also started from a blank chalkboard. There were very few Mandarin speakers among Singapore's Chinese population in the 1960s. Chinese Singaporeans of that era mostly spoke in Chinese dialects and, if educated, probably good English, or Malay. Following the breakaway from the Malaysian Federation and the founding of the Republic of Singapore in 1965, the Singapore government began implementing a draconian language policy in the late 1970s which emphasized bi-lingual education in English and choosing a 2nd language either being Mandarin, Tamil, or Malay.[9] Owing to Singapore's delicate geo-political status nestled

[8] Source: *South China Morning Post* in November 2015 published information citing results from a Swedish training group, EF English First, noting Hong Kong's global ranking in English proficiency among secondary school students had fallen from 12th in 2011 to 33rd among 70 countries in 2015. Accusations abound over the reason for this decline.

[9] Singapore's population is approximately 76% ethnic Chinese, 15% Malay, and 7% Subcontinent Indian. The Singapore language bi-lingual policy requires students to choose English and one other language (Mandarin, Malay, or Tamil) as their two languages of bi-lingual study. Given the rise of China in global trade, many Singaporeans choose Mandarin as their second language regardless of their race.

between Malaysia and Indonesia, Singapore decided to maintain Malay under its constitution as the official national language of Singapore.[10] However, government leadership under Prime Minister Lew Kuan-Yew considered it to be essential for Singaporeans to have bi-lingual language skills in English and Mandarin in order to thrive in the global economy in the Twenty-First Century. Few critics can argue that this policy has been off the mark. It has resulted in Singapore providing a modern-day workforce that has high level of competency in both English and Mandarin. It is especially attractive for multi-national corporations operating offices and factories in Asia to recruit young, educated Singaporeans owing to their proven language skills. In summary, vis-à-vis competition from mainland Chinese students, Taiwanese, Singaporeans, and Malaysian Chinese, the Hong Kong government may need to re-assess how well they are preparing young Hong Kong graduates for job opportunities in the new global economy.

Beyond the controversial language competency issue the teaching of Chinese history to Hong Kong youth has also impacted Hong Kong's social integration into Greater China as well. Through the end of 2017, a full 20 years after the 1997 handover, Hong Kong schools were still not universally requiring schools to teach Chinese history covering certain modern periods after the 1911 fall of the Qing Dynasty. The interpretation of Chinese history following 1911 has been subject to multiple interpretations by historians and no doubt a headache for educators in Hong Kong tasked with setting textbook policy. Prior to 1997, the 1966–1967 Hong Kong riots were still not being covered in Hong Kong history classes, a full 30 years after the fact. It is no wonder that on Hong Kong streets today that many young Hong Kongers are claiming that they are not Chinese. This is an identity crisis. It is a great irony because many of the parents and grandparents who fled China in 1949 and resurrected their lives in Hong Kong do consider themselves Chinese. The challenge for the Hong Kong government going forward will be to help mold a Hong Kong identity for the Twenty-First Century, allowing for its uniqueness but defining it within the context of being Chinese and a part of the Greater Bay Area.

[10] Malay is the official language of Malaysia, the nation of 32 million inhabitants to Singapore's north, and almost identical to Bahasa Indonesian which is the official language of Indonesia, the archipelago nation of 264 million inhabitants directly located to Singapore's south.

The Future Hong Kong Model: Becoming like Switzerland or the Former Yugoslavia?

Digressing a bit from the discussion about Hong Kong identity it might be useful to examine two other country models that have historically diverse ethnic and linguistic make-up. Let's look at Switzerland and the former Yugoslavia. Switzerland is a vibrant and affluent country of 8.5 million citizens that recognizes four official languages: German, French, Italian, and Romanish. While two-thirds of Swiss are native German speakers, the German that they speak varies in accent dramatically from Zurich to Basel to the capital city of Berne.[11] Native French speakers are found in the western areas of the country in Geneva and Neuchatel and Lausanne. Native Italian speakers are found mainly in southeastern Switzerland in the small cities of Lugano, Locarno, and Bellinzona. Romansh, only spoken by a small number of Swiss largely in the canton of Grisons (Graubunden), is still recognized as one of the four official languages. Within the Swiss educational system, students are required to learn more than one language. In fact, if you meet an educated Swiss on the streets today, you will likely find someone who speaks three languages, usually two of the Swiss recognized languages and also English. Many Swiss, in fact, communicate with each other in English in business settings and many Swiss companies (particularly those seeking to compete in the international arena) have adopted English as their corporate language. The business school IMD based in Lausanne, generally recognized as one of the top business schools in the world, conducts its classes in English. Swiss are passionately patriotic no matter whether they are Swiss German, Francophone Swiss, or Italian Swiss. One does not normally find a German speaking Swiss citizen who says "I am German" or "I am not Swiss."

Then there is the model of the former Yugoslavia which was formally part of the former Austria-Hungarian Empire. Its capital city, Vienna,

[11] The writer posits that the language that most resembles the nuances in Chinese in grammatical and linguistic similarity is German. German speakers mostly read the same written German. However, Swiss German, Austrian German, Bavarian German, and High German differ dramatically in sound. Most German speakers study High German (or Hochdeutsch) which is the dialect spoken in north, central Germany. It would be the dialect taught in schools in Germany, Switzerland, and Austria i.e. the equivalent to Mandarin in the world of Chinese speakers.

was considered the cultural center of Europe for most of the Nineteenth Century under Habsburg Dynastic rule.

However, Austria-Hungary sadly could not survive the competition between Great Powers in the Nineteenth Century and the outbreak of World War I that occurred following the assassination of Archduke Ferdinand and his wife in the city of Sarajevo in June 1914. Following the conclusion of World War I and the Paris Peace Conference and subsequent Treaty of Versailles (1919), Austria-Hungary became dissolved, severed and spun off into a series of "balkanized" republics.[12] Yugoslavia, with a capital set up at Belgrade, became one of the republics.

Yugoslavia inherited many of the old Austria-Hungarian problems and, like China, consisted of many different ethnic groups, diverse mother tongues, and religions. The Balkan states that emerged after World War I and survived World War II into the modern era were never able to stay unified. Yugoslavia did hold together remarkably under the 37 year rule of charismatic leader of Josip Tito until 1980.[13] However, the country became torn apart in the 1990s by ethnic strife. The tripwire to disunity and disintegration were the economic problems that eventually enveloped them. Economic distress and nativism led to internal ethnic and religiously driven strife and eventual disintegration in the early 1990s and a war that killed an estimated 130,000 citizens. Hong Kong must avoid in its society the example of the Balkans. "One country, two systems" requires a well-educated, resilient, and broadly cohesive population where all segments of society feel franchised. Creating a platform for fair competition in all areas of the economy allows for talent and ambition to achieve wealth and productivity gains. Hyper emphasis on economic development carries the risk of imbalances in other areas. Accordingly, proper distribution of wealth and creating inclusiveness in the society must also be equally important priorities that address the self-destructive risks of a widening income gap.

[12] Among the republics that emerged after World War 1 were Czechoslovakia, Hungary, and Yugoslavia.

[13] The city of Sarajevo even hosted the Winter Olympics in 1984. Sarajevo was part of the former Yugoslavia and later broke off to become capital of Bosnia and Herzegovina. The 1984 Winter Olympic stadium in Sarajevo has been converted into a cemetery for 11,500 local residents who perished in the 1990s conflict including over 1500 children.

Epilogue: Heading Toward a New Paradigm

> I am going into all of this, because a student of history will understand that the Chinese psyche has heavy baggage when it comes to any threat, foreign or domestic, to carve up Chinese territories. When the topic of any separatist movement comes up, Chinese people feel a strong sense of shame and anger because of this history of foreign occupation. The one thing that is terribly misunderstood, and often ignored, by the western press and those critical of China is that 1.4 billion Chinese citizens stand united when it comes to the territorial integrity of China and the country's sovereignty over her homeland. This issue is non-negotiable.
>
> —Joseph Tsai, Owner of Brooklyn Nets NBA team Owner

I noted with respect the comments made by NBA Brooklyn Nets owner, Joseph Tsai, in the aftermath of controversial comments made off-the-cuff in late 2019 by the general manager of another NBA team about the Hong Kong protests. I knew Joe's father professionally in Taiwan years ago when I worked and lived there. The Tsai family history reads like the story tale of many Chinese families during the past century. His father's family escaped the chaos and disruption in mainland China during the 1949 revolution and then re-established the family home in Taiwan. Joe's father co-founded a law firm in Taipei and was well known throughout the local Taiwan business community for his reliable legal expertise. Following an early childhood growing up in Taiwan, Joe's parents sent him to the United States as a teenager to further his education initially at the

B. VonCannon, *Status Anxiety*,
https://doi.org/10.1007/978-981-15-7028-5

Lawrenceville School in New Jersey and then to Yale University. Joe was an outstanding student and an accomplished two-sport athlete. In fact, he played linebacker on his high school football team and he continued varsity sports at Yale where he earned both a B.A. degree and later a law degree.

Joe's success in the commercial world reads like a fairytale as he became a co-founder of Alibaba Inc., one of China's major success stories in the corporate world and key player in the world of internet technology and e-commerce. Following his success in the business world Joe began to realize his dream to own a professional sports team. He eventually became the new owner of the NBA Brooklyn Nets in 2018. Joe's comments on the Hong Kong issue do not surprise me. He echoes the sentiments of many Chinese, even those families who fled the Communist regime in the 1940s. Whether they live in Chinese communities in Southeast Asia, North America, or Europe, the overwhelming majority of ethnic Chinese around the globe harbor a strong sense of loyalty over China's sovereignty and its right to territorial integrity.

I remain convinced that the current challenge in Hong Kong has been caused by a growing income gap problem in Hong Kong more than any other factor. The Hong Kong protests have more in common with the "Make America Great Again" and "Gilets Jaunes" phenomena in the United States and France than a classic 1776 "Give me liberty or give me death" struggle. While there are certainly dedicated human rights activists in Hong Kong who seek to make the current crisis uniquely a "pro-democracy movement," I remain unconvinced that "lack of democracy" is the chief cause of the protests. With such a large number of protestors aged under the age of 18 participating in the protests, it suggests to me that a level of teenage coercion has occurred. Statistics through the end of 2019 show that nearly 40% of the protestors are under the age of 24 and a full 25% arrested under the age of 18.

I lament the clear evidence that some of the protests have been funded by offshore interests. Reliable stories have documented episodes of young students being paid to throw Molotov cocktails and vandalize public and private property. Young students who wear Googles, tear gas mufflers, and helmets are sporting equipment that in many instances cost in excess of USD 250—clearly beyond a student's budget. Someone has been placing Union Jack and Stars and Stripes flags in the hands of the youth—something particularly revolting to many older generation Chinese who live in Hong Kong. Rumors persist that non-governmental organizations (commonly called "NGOs") have backed the protests and the names on this list of possible offshore sponsors range from private groups like National Endowment for Democracy (NED) in the U.S., to private groups from Taiwan, to anti-Beijing mainlander dissident groups living outside of mainland China. If this is true, over time the truth will be known. They who seek to hijack and expand the Hong Kong problem into a broader geo-political issue will be disclosed in due course. It is my hope that this outside intervention will cease.

The Hong Kong police force has become the target of much criticism by the western media. In my view, they are the most well-trained and disciplined police force in Asia.

Widespread claims of police brutality have been leveled at the police force. However, on the ground in Hong Kong it is extraordinary witnessing procedurally how the police have raised flags (yes, banners with written warnings) on most occasions before they have used tear gas (giving protesters and particularly the young students under 18 a chance to disperse). In what other country is such a dignified and polite manner of using force deployed? Of course, with such frequent and heightened levels of violence there have been instances and isolated cases of police going outside the normal bounds of behavior and failing to observe standard procedures. However, the police department has regularly given press conferences to explain their actions. In an attempt to maintain transparency to the broader Hong Kong population, they have openly admitted when they have taken action to apply discipline internally members of their own police force. Quite likely whatever degree of self-discipline the police force applies to themselves internally will never be enough and suitable in the eyes of the most radical factions within the Hong Kong protest movement or certain western journalists and human rights groups. The Hong Kong police have been called upon to cope with extraordinary levels of street violence throughout many areas of the city. Unlike policemen in Western countries who are licensed to carry guns and use them when threatened, many Hong Kong police do not carry deadly weapons. My club tennis team competes each year in local Hong Kong sports competition with one of the police clubs and we have always considered them to be among Hong Kong's finest citizens. As sportsmen they competed fairly and exhibited the highest standards of sportsmanship. However, over the past six months of street unrest they have become the object of much ridicule which I think is largely undeserved. When one considers the level of violence in streets in Hong Kong through the end of

Table 1 U.S. Chamber China Conference 2018: Areas of greatest opportunity

Six areas of greatest opportunity	
• Healthcare and Biotech	74%
• Artificial Intelligence	67%
• Blockchain Technology	45%
• E-Commerce	25%
• Education	21%
• Mobility/Logistics	10%

Source These were the six categories with most opportunity for collaboration and mutual opportunity ranked by U.S. executives attending the American Chamber of Commerce forum in Hong Kong in late 2018

2019, were such vandalism to have occurred in any North American city, it is my estimation that mortality rates for protestors in a Western urban setting would surely have been much higher than the level of injury that has occurred in Hong Kong.

I remain hopeful that Sino-US trade relations which have enjoyed an expanding and comprehensive path dating from a starting point back in the 1970s at the end of the Cold War will get back on track. The new reality is that the U.S. and China will inevitably become strategic competitors. For nearly 40 years emphasizing "pragmatism over ideology" has been the glue that has held Sino-U.S. trade ties together rather than resorting to the old Cold War style of both sides seeking to re-make each other's internal politics. The U.S. will no doubt continue press China trade officials to give evidence that they are enforcing intellectual property rights (IPR) as well as guaranteeing continued opening and fair access to China's domestic market in the product goods and service industries. These key issues must continue to be addressed or otherwise they become the fuel of "nativist" groups within the U.S. who oppose global trade. The scope of the shared interests of the U.S. and China remains very broad (see Table 1) and keeping shared economic interests as a priority will set the pace for more stability and wealth creation globally. A 2018 study released by the American Chamber in Commerce in Hong Kong where most regional CEOs are based highlighted the major areas where American company senior managers say great opportunity for cooperation and collaboration with Chinese corporations and institutions.

The enemy of this happening, of course, are regrettably the far right-wing groups not only in the United States but also some in Great Britain and continental European countries who are guided by a Manichean approach[1] to China (We are good, they are evil!) and as a mantra for guiding relationships outside their country. For the U.S. and China to fall into a 1960s style U.S vs. Soviet Union type Cold War would be wantonly unwise and a step backward for human history. Since the early 1980s China has advanced over 800 million people out of poverty in a period of less than 40 years. Western analysts need to stop pontificating and making value judgements about how China governs itself internally and take note of the policies that have enabled people to rise out of poverty and uneducated squalor to become part of an inclusive middle class which will soon be larger than the entire U.S. population. For all of China's perceived shortcomings in foreign policy, they have not invaded any other country since the Sino-Vietnamese skirmishes of 1979. Home ownership in China today is at 84%, slightly above that of the United States (62%) and at such level much higher than the current level of home ownership in Hong Kong.[2] Nearly 100% of China's population are covered by universal healthcare compared to the United States where, despite superior hospital facilities and world renown medical specialists, over 27.5 million people have no health insurance.[3] At its current pace of growth, the size of China's economy will likely overtake that of the United States within the coming decade. This does not need to be viewed with envy. China and India today account for one third of the global population. Smaller countries around the world benefit when these two large countries' economies along with the that of the United States serve as they have in the past as the engines of global GDP growth.

Seeking to create open markets for goods and services rather than erecting more tariffs should be the ultimate goal. While Sino-U.S. trade negotiations will continue to be necessary and sometimes result in differences, it is critical to avoid a breakdown in the global trading system. The advent of a 1930s style global trade war would inevitably move the world

[1] Credit for coining this term, "Manichean approach," is due to Harvard professor, Dr. William Overholt, in "Crisis of Success" (2019). It refers to the ancient philosophy of Manichaeism which sought to break everything down into good and evil based the teachings of prophet Mani who lived in Persia in the Third Century A.D.

[2] This statistic featured in "China's Crisis of Success" (2019) by William H. Overholt of Harvard University.

[3] Latest figure provided by September 2019 article in Wall Street Journal by Stephanie Armour's article "Number of Uninsured Americans Rises for First Time in Decade".

toward declining living standards and risk of military conflict. It is also critical to avoid a new arms race. The U.S. easily outpaced the old Soviet Union under the Reagan Administration in the 1980s as its economy was 10 times larger than the Soviet economy. Today China's economy is currently only slightly smaller than the U.S. economy and its population is four times larger than the U.S. population. A new Cold War would be catastrophic for both countries and the entire world.

Potential exists for Hong Kong to remain significant and as a facilitator between East and West. Hong Kong's great blessing is its geographical proximity to Guangdong Province and growing integration into the Greater Bay Area combined with the 230 year history of "soft skills" retained by its highly resilient and industrious Cantonese population. These soft skills can erode if not enhanced through educational initiatives but they are not easily duplicated. The economic factors show spillover effect into Hong Kong's economy from China's growth since 1980 to be unmistakable. Street protestors and journalists who seek to espouse theories that China's economic rise spells Hong Kong's downfall are only spreading half-truths. See GDP figures dating from 1980 in Table 2.

Hong Kong, being the quintessential free trade port on the planet, has a continued important role to play in the process of promoting trade and raising capital for both investors and users of capital. Despite the outbreak of street violence, the ugly episodes of nativist chauvinism, the offshore meddling, and ominous threat of prolonged trade wars, I remain optimistic about Hong Kong. In the words of Dr. Victor Fung who chaired the recent "2022 Foundation"[4] as well as serving as past chairman of the Greater Pearl River Delta Business Council, "Hong Kong's signature strength through different times and challenges has been an ability to reinvent itself. I see the GBA as a reason for Hong Kong to reinvent itself yet again. This next iteration is more nuanced than morphing from export manufacturing to international services, as Hong Kong did after the PRD's first opening 40 years ago. Hong Kong is, after all, already a highly developed, sophisticated economy. That being said, this newest iteration is set to be every bit as transformative as the previous one, and just as significant globally." The findings of the 2022 Foundation

[4]The non-profit 2022 Foundation has produced numerous studies on Hong Kong's long-term competitiveness since 1997 and most recently completed a study led by Dr. Michael J. Enright entitled "Creating the Greater Bay Area of the Future- Opportunities for Hong Kong" (2019).

Table 2 Hong Kong GDP growth in U.S. dollars since 1980

Hong Kong GDP—Historical data

Year	*GDP*	*Per capita*	*Growth (%)*
2018	$362.99B	$48,717	3.02
2017	$341.65B	$46,221	3.84
2016	$320.86B	$43,734	2.18
2015	$309.38B	$42,432	2.39
2014	$291.46B	$40,315	2.76
2013	$275.70B	$38,404	3.10
2012	$262.63B	$36,731	1.70
2011	$248.518	$35,142	4.81
2010	$228.64B	$32,550	6.77
2009	$214.05B	$30,697	−2.46
2008	$219.28B	$31,516	2.13
2007	$211.60B	$30,594	6.46
2006	S193.54B	$28,224	7.03
2005	S181.57B	$26,650	7.39
2004	S169.10B	$24,928	8.70
2003	$161.38B	$23,977	3.06
2002	$166.35B	$24,666	1.66
2001	$169.40B	$25,230	0.56
2000	$171.67B	$25,757	7.66
1999	S165.77B	$25,092	2.51
1998	$168.89B	$25,809	−5.88
1997	$177.35B	$27,330	5.10
1996	$159.72B	$24,818	4.26
1995	$144.65B	$23,497	2.37
1994	$135.81B	$22,503	6.04
1993	$120.35B	$20,396	6.20
1992	$104.27B	$17,976	6.24
1991	$88.96B	$15,466	5.70
1990	$76.93B	$13,486	3.83
1989	$68.79B	$12,098	2.28
1988	$59.71B	$10,610	8.51
1987	$50.62B	$9071	13.40
1986	$41.08B	$7435	11.06
1985	$35.70B	$6543	0.76
1984	$33.51B	$6208	9.97
1983	$29.91B	$5595	5.98
1982	$32.29B	$6134	2.95
1981	$31.06B	$5991	9.26
1980	$28.86B	$5700	10.11

Source Macrotrends

Table 3 The 11 city constellation within the GBA

City	*Brief description of role within GBA*
Hong Kong	Smart city: the pivot point for companies entering GBA market
Guangzhou	Capital city, admin, marketing, retail, and distribution center
Shenzhen	High tech manufacturing, research, and development
Macao	Leading resort and global casino no 1 and linked to Zhuhai
Dongguan	Upgrade to higher value manufacturing (electronics, IOT)
Foshan	Upgrade to smart manufacturing like robotics/automation
Zhuhai	Service center for manufacturers in west GBA and tourism
Zhongshan	Advanced manufacturing focus and trade financing platform
Huizhou	Outer ring of GBA city and heavy industry base
Zhaoqing	Outer ring city and recipient of migration from GBA inner ring
Jiangmen	Outer ring city and recipient of manufacturing migration

Source 2022 Foundation (2019)

also call for Hong Kong's role to morph from that of a "hub" for the Pearl River Basin to that as part of a constellation of 11 cities in the GBA that are linked as a network with each node contributing its particular area of specialization. It should be added that it is not only easy to foresee that Hong Kong's role is changing but the role of each major city within GBA is changing. Transportation links and connectivity enhancements have created the opportunity for the "inner ring" of GBA cities to evolve to new areas of specialization while passing manufacturing to "outer ring cities" like Huizhou, Zhaoqing, and Jiangmen. These areas of specialization are briefly outlined in Table 3.

The culmination of six months of unrest on the streets of Hong Kong in the second half of 2019 were clearly subjecting Hong Kong to a deteriorating economic situation by year's end. Hong Kong's annual GDP contracted by 1.2% in 2019 for the first time in ten years after it had actually registered positive growth in the first six months of the year. Despite this setback I believe fervently the people of Hong Kong will emerge even stronger from this temporary moment of status anxiety and identity crisis.

Time and time again Hong Kong has risen to the occasion. The latest coronavirus health crisis which descended upon the Hong Kong suddenly in early 2020 with all its somber threat to daily life actually has given hope to many that the benevolent side of Hong Kong society and a civic unity will come forth. Many residents had not forgotten the harrowing experience of the Severe Acute Respiratory Syndrome (SARS) epidemic in the spring of 2003 which spread throughout Asia after initial detection in northern China. SARS nearly brought the Hong Kong economy to a standstill in the spring of that year with real estate prices dropping as much as 50% in some areas of the city and companies mandating work-from-home policies. A much higher mortality rate was observed in SARS patients (15–20% compared to a current estimated 5% for Covid-19). Numbers of infected in Hong Kong that year reached approximately 1800 with a death toll approaching 300. Fortunately drugs that could successfully treat SARS were quickly discovered which does not seem to be the case at the outset as the Covid-19 virus spreads across the globe 17 years later. The SARS crisis in Hong Kong proved to be a wake up call for government health and sanitation departments to raise standards dramatically. It has also conditioned Hong Kongers in the latest fight against Covid-19. Remarkably Hong Kongers, no matter their political persuasion, have observed an informal truce in the fight against the coronavirus.

While there have been a few sporadic marches by protestors and grousing from activists continues in local TV interviews, there has been a general respect for the seriousness of the moment and the health risks presented by the Covid-19 pandemic. Government authorities attempting to implement "social distancing" measures aimed at curbing the spread of Covid-19 have banned public assembly of more than four persons. Street violence has at least temporarily subsided. Students can be seen handing out face masks to the elderly or delivering food to the residences of the needy. Wearing a face mask in public has been encouraged by authorities in stark contrast to a two week period at the height of the protests in the previous autumn when wearing a mask was increasing deemed as symbol of defiance against the government. Now mask wearing has become among Hong Kongers a symbol of unity in the fight against the coronavirus. Hong Kongers are united in this fight against a common enemy. To date into the 10th week following the government's closure of schools across the special administrative region in mid-January, the facts and figures speak for themselves.[5] Hong Kongers of all walks of life have banded together to confront this unprecedented health crisis. As the Covid-19 pandemic spread outside of Greater China into Asian countries in February and began ravaging through parts of Europe and the United

[5] Statistics released by public health authorities in Hong Kong through mid-April 2020 showed Covid-19 infections to be just under 1014 and less than 10 deaths.

States, the people of Hong Kong deserved an accolade for their resilience and determination to control the virus. Hong Kong had joined the list of global leaders like Taiwan, and South Korea who were rising to the challenge and role models for other countries in the battle to control the spread of Covid-19.

The attributes that enabled a spartan post-1949 Hong Kong society to make remarkable advances and achieve staggering levels of wealth accumulation relate directly to its strong sense of local Cantonese pride. Living in the memory of the death and destruction of the Japanese occupation and internment camps on Hong Kong soil (1942–1945) and the painful post-World War II recovery and widespread separation of families during the 1949 revolution, the people of Hong Kong pushed forward because they were humble and industrious. Practically within earshot of the chaos and lawlessness of the Cultural Revolution on the mainland in the 1960s, Hong Kong citizens remained stoic and were law abiding and pushed forward. Victoria Harbor in Hong Kong in the 1950–1960s time period became the oriental equivalent of what New York harbor and the Statue of Liberty stood for in early Twentieth Century America—"Give me your tired, your poor, your huddled masses…." Hong Kong of that period was tolerant and rejoiced in its cultural diversity. The Hong Kong of that era was an "against all odds" good bet and welcomed competition. That spirit is missing today but it is not too late to re-kindle it.

All Hong Kongers must also realize there is no going back to the past. While economic progress can continue, Hong Kong will never return to the days when it comprised nearly 27% of China's GDP like in the 1990s. It will never enjoy a near monopoly on China trade like existed for Guangdong Province under the Qing Dynasty or Hong Kong during post World War II British Colonial rule. Embracing cultural integration opportunities within the Greater Bay Area (GBA) today by Hong Kong ensures it remains relevant in the expansion of greater regional economic activity that can potentially create jobs and prosperity for citizens of Hong Kong. To achieve this vision of the new Hong Kong identity, Hong Kongers must not only be bi-lingual, they need to embrace multi-lingual training assiduously and become more like the multi-lingual Swiss than remaining frozen, inward looking (and risk suffering the fate of the Balkans). More training and adjustments in the Hong Kong education system will need to be made that will program Hong Kong youth for success in a globally competitive job market. Hong Kong's economy today is 92% dependent upon service industry sectors[6] and has evolved fundamentally from the 1980s style economy that it was when manufacturing composed over 46% of Hong Kong's GDP. A key challenge in the days ahead for the core stakeholders in Hong Kong society, that is the children, the parents, the educators, and the government leaders is that of ensuring Hong Kong youth can be weaned away from self-destructive violence and be taught to be "Hong Kong proud" and "Chinese proud." The two are not mutually exclusive. Sacrifices to the current or past status quo will be necessary. In the search for a new identity there is no going back.

[6] Figures released by HK Census and Statistics Dept in 2016 showed that service industries including financial services, professional services (legal, accounting), trade related services, and tourism accounted for nearly 57% of Hong Kong's GDP (Source: 2022 Foundation Report [2019]).

Index

B. VonCannon, *Status Anxiety*,
https://doi.org/10.1007/978-981-15-7028-5

CPSIA information can be obtained
at www.ICGtesting.com
Printed in the USA
LVHW081932210221
679567LV00008B/823

9 789811 570278